*Motorbooks International*
**WARBIRD HISTORY**

# B-25 MITCHELL

Steve Pace

*In memory of James H. Doolittle, 1896–1993, who became a national hero when he led the first World War II bombing raid on Japan at the controls of a North American B-25B Mitchell on 18 April 1942.*

First published in 1994 by Motorbooks International Publishers & Wholesalers, PO Box 2, 729 Prospect Avenue, Osceola, WI 54020 USA

© Steve Pace, 1994

Motorbooks International is a certified trademark, registered with the United States Patent Office

The information in this book is true and complete to the best of our knowledge. All recommendations are made without any guarantee on the part of the author or Publisher, who also disclaim any liability incurred in connection with the use of this data or specific details

We recognize that some words, model names and designations, for example, mentioned herein are the property of the trademark holder. We use them for identification purposes only. This is not an official publication

Motorbooks International books are also available at discounts in bulk quantity for industrial or sales-promotional use. For details write to Special Sales Manager at the Publisher's address

Library of Congress Cataloging-in-Publication Data

Pace, Steve.
    B-25 Mitchell/Steve Pace.
        p. cm.
    Includes bibliographical references and index.
    ISBN 0-87938-939-7
    1. Mitchell bomber—History. 2. World War, 1939-1945—Aerial operations, American. I. Title.
    UG1242.B6P32          1994
    358.4'2—dc20          94-23268

Printed in Hong Kong

**On the front cover:** "Bones," the 1,000th and last B-25H produced at North American's Inglewood plant (USAAF serial number 43-5104), was the last California-built Mitchell. Covered with the autographs of the men and women who built her, "Bones" became one of fifteen other B-25s of the 81st BS, 12th bomber group and served until VJ-Day without ever receiving a standard paint job. *Rockwell*

**On the title page:** A glass–nose B-25J of the 12th bomber group in the CBI Theater of Operations is prepared for its next mission; this J being based in India (unknown squadron). *Hank Redmond via J. Ethell*

# Contents

Walt Spivak joined North American Aviation, Incorporated, in 1936 as a draftsman. He first worked on the BT-9 basic trainer and later the XB-21 bomber. When the contract was received to build the NA-40 attack bomber (the predecessor of the B-25), he was in charge of the group that engineered its fuselage and armament system. In 1940, Spivak became project engineer on the B-25 program. After the war ended in Europe, Spivak became more and more involved in the higher echelons of North American Aviation while working on notable aircraft programs such as the F-82 Twin Mustang, B-45 Tornado, A-2 Savage, F-86 Sabre Jet, F-1 Fury, F-100 Super Sabre, A-5 Vigilante, X-15, B-70 Valkyrie, and the B-1 Lancer, among many others. Holding the title of senior consultant to Rockwell International Corporation, North American Aircraft, he retired in 1984. *Rockwell*

# Acknowledgments

I would like to give my deepest thanks to the following individuals for their time and effort in helping me prepare this reference: Chris Wamsley, Rockwell International Corporation; Walt Spivak (retired) and Norm Avery (retired), Rockwell International Corporation, North American Aircraft; Mrs. Cheryl Gumm, AFFTC/HO, Edwards AFB; John M. and Donna Campbell, Campbell Archives; Jeff Ethell; Dave Menard; Vic Tatelman; Robert F. Dorr; Bill Hess; Larry Hickey; Doug Spawn; Tony Landis; Alex Adair; Bob Wilson; Carl Wildner; Charlie Bright; Fred Corning; Ernest McDowell; R. T. Smith; Charles Baisden; Greg Field, Lee Klancher, Zack Miller, Bobbi Jones, and the rest of the friendly and hard-working editorial staff at Motorbooks International.

# Foreword

The B-25 was my first production airplane at North American Aviation, Inc. It moved from a proposal to 184 production airplanes in a very short time. I was still a young airplane designer, but I gathered a lot of experience from two twin-engined airplanes designed and developed at North American—the NA-39 (XB-21), a midwing bomber for high altitude operations, and the NA-40 (no military designation), a high-wing attack airplane with dual vertical tails. One of the features of the NA-40 attack airplane was its underslung engine nacelles that gave it low drag and high propulsive efficiency.

I began the B-25 (NA-62) program under Carl J. "Red" Hansen, a project engineer. I was design group leader on the fuselage and assistant project engineer. As the program increased in tempo and the war got into high gear, Red Hansen moved up in the organization and I took his place as B-25 project engineer.

The first flight of the first B-25 was in August 1940, just a year after its program starting date. By that time we were in full-scale production on the first 184 airplanes: twenty-four B-25s, forty B-25As, and 120 B-25Bs. In September 1940, just a month after the first flight of the number one B-25, we got a contract for 863 B-25C airplanes.

Many more contracts followed for the B-25D, B-25G, B-25H, B-25J, and PBJ Mitchells. Overnight, almost literally, we were on our way to a very successful airplane production program.

North American Aviation had to expand fast to handle all the aircraft the war effort required. When the Doolittle raid on Tokyo was announced, there was a great increase in employee morale—especially among those working on the B-25.

Since most of the B-25s were scheduled to be built in the new Kansas City plant, I was transferred to Kansas in December 1943 as chief engineer. Kansas was a new experience for me. The engineering force was decreasing because the Draft Board was picking up all of our younger men, and replacements were badly needed. We started up a program with the University of Kansas to train young women in design and drafting. An eight-week course was started, and a new one began every two weeks with thirty women in every class. It turned out to be a very good program.

We ultimately got up to a production rate of thirteen Mitchells a day; that was a lot of airplanes. I stayed with the B-25 program until the end of the war in Europe and helped to close down the Kansas City plant in late 1945 before I returned to the Inglewood plant in California.

As an aside, we at the Kansas City plant manufactured a total of 6,608 B-25 and PBJ airplanes at an average rate of 157 airplanes every full month our plant was making deliveries; peak employment was 28,130 persons at work in October 1943.

As chief engineer, my experience with the B-25 was both challenging and rewarding.

*Walter A. Spivak*

# Introduction

Piston-powered and propeller-driven, the twin-engined and twin-tailed B-25 Mitchell is considered by many as the most successful medium-class bomber to do battle in World War II. First ordered into production in September 1939, North American Aviation, Inc., manufactured 9,889 B-25 and PBJ airplanes from August 1940 to October 1945 at plants in Inglewood, California, and Kansas City, Kansas.

Conceived while war clouds rapidly gathered over Europe and developed while German land and air forces were finding little opposition on that continent, the Air Force's B-25 and the Navy's PBJ were in continuous production for sixty months, during which these fly-away airplanes and 1,340 equivalent airplanes in spare parts were delivered to the US Air Forces, Allies, and friends.

From the dramatic carrier-launched attack on Japan early in World War II to the day-after-day combat missions against the Axis powers, the thousands of B-25 and PBJ bomber planes played a significant role. The Mitchell bombers amply justified the warm respect of the brave crews that manned them and the lasting pride of the thousands of men and women who designed, developed, and built them.

The legendary B-25 helped prove the philosophy of its namesake, William S. "Billy" Mitchell, one of the first and best-known military advocates for a strong air arm in the United States.

Official testimony to the versatility of the B-25 was contained in a statement by Assistant Secretary of War Robert A. Lovett published late in 1943:

There are few more dramatic examples of the advantages of combat improvement of current [airplane] models than the modifications and design changes to the B-25 medium bomber. It is serving in every theater of war all around the world. For example, already a superb medium bomber, the Fifth Air Force in the Southwest Pacific, working with North American Aviation, Inc., has converted it into a devastating attack bomber with tremendous fire power forward and a specialized technique in medium-altitude bombing of shipping.

The North American B-25 Mitchell was developed to serve as a dedicated medium-class bomber. As often happens, however, it was continuously redesigned and modified to perform a number of additional roles. These added duties included advanced trainer, attack bomber, mapping and photographic reconnaissance, transport, radar and fire control trainer, and patrol bomber to hunt and kill submarines.

The B-25 was an instant winner among its bombardment pilots and it quickly established North American as a dynamic entity in the design and development of advanced aircraft. As a war machine it was well received, reliable, and respected by its crew members. As one result of its success, the B-25 effectively demonstrated the air power its namesake had believed in.

This is the story of the Billy Mitchell.

US Army Air Corps Maj. Gen. William S. "Billy" Mitchell, one of America's premier architects of US air power, appears to materialize with his B-25 namesake. *Rockwell*

Chapter 1

# Genesis

To find an advanced replacement for the Douglas B-18 Bolo—a twin-engine medium-class bomber based on the Douglas DC-2 commercial airliner—the US Army Air Corps (USAAC) on 11 March 1939 issued Circular Proposal (CP) Number 39-640 to the industry. Subsequently on 30 June 1939, North American Aviation, Inc., (NAA) submitted a bid in response to CP No. 39-640. Included within its bid, NAA offered a total of eighty-one different twin-engine medium-class bombardment airplane design configurations. Monetary bids were opened on 5 July 1939 at Wright Army Air Field near Dayton, Ohio. North American was later notified by letter that it was one of two successful bidders on CP No. 39-640. The other successful bid came from Martin. A contract calling for the production of 184 airplanes to be known as the B-25 type

Edgar Schmued (left), Dutch Kindleberger (center), and Lee Atwood in a late 1940s freeze frame. Schmued was one of America's most successful aircraft designers; Kindleberger was NAA's first president; and Atwood, former NAA vice president and chief engineer and later president and chairman of the board, was most instrumental in the merger of NAA and Rockwell International Corporation in 1967. If not for these three men—especially—and many others, the B-25 would have never materialized. *Rockwell*

was approved for NAA on 20 September 1939. Another contract ordering 201 airplanes to be known as the B-26 type was simultaneously awarded to Martin.

## Initial Development

Prior to contract approval, NAA had already begun its detail engineering and had issued construction orders to its experimental shop—a relatively small area within its Inglewood, California, factory where any new type of plane would be, for the most part, built by hand under stringent security measures. The first engineering hours were charged to the bomber's development on 12 August 1939. Construction of 184 NA-62 (B-25 type) airplanes and a single static structural proof loads test airframe was authorized on 5 September. The release date for engineering drawings to NAA's X-shop was 13 April 1940. Initial development of the B-25 required some 8,500 design drawings and about 200,000 engineering hours. The first B-25 was completed on 6 August 1940, and on the same day, it entered engine evaluations.

Prior to the development of the B-25 type bomber, the experience of NAA with twin-engine aircraft had been limited to two experimental types. The first of these being NAA's NA-21, developed several years earlier.

## The NA-21

On April Fool's Day in 1936, the US-AAC initiated a top-priority program to

acquire a modern medium-class twin-engine bomber. With approval of then USAAC commander Maj. Gen. Oscar Westover, the USAAC issued CP Number 36-528 to the industry.

In part, that circular proposal required that the bomber would have the attributes as follows:

• A combat range of 2,000 miles with a 2,200lb bomb load (two 1,100lb bombs), or a combat range of 660 miles with an 8,800lb bomb load (eight 1,100lb bombs); adequate armament for full-perimeter self-defense.

• Accommodations for a five-man crew: pilot, copilot, bombardier/navigator, radio operator/gunner, and gunner.

• A top speed of 225mph at best operating altitude or at the desired altitude of 25,000ft.

• Be of a midwing monoplane (single-wing) design, with all-metal construction and retractable landing gear.

• Be propelled by two air-cooled turbosupercharged radial engines, optimized for high altitude operation, with as much takeoff horsepower as possible.

Daunting as these requirements were in 1936, airframe and powerplant technologies in the United States had matured enough that the requirements were not impossible to deal with. Thus in their respective efforts to generate new monies and jobs during that era of depression, most airframe contractors

11

Looking northwest this view of NAA's Inglewood factory, next to Mines Field (now LAX), was photographed in the late 1930s. Surrounded by Los Angeles (above), Inglewood (below), El Segundo and Hawthorne (left and lower left), the nearly new factory was accessed by Imperial Highway (left) and Aviation Boulevard (bottom). Look closely and you will see the XB-21 "Dragon" bomber to the right of the factory. *Rockwell*

came up with offerings for the circular proposal. These airframe contractors included Boeing, Douglas, Lockheed, Martin, and North American. Boeing, Douglas, and Martin, already having a great deal of experience in the design and manufacturing processes of bombardment-type aircraft, were the immediate front-runners. But NAA, having never produced a bombardment airplane before, still offered a design that met US-AAC requirements; and it was not ignored. In fact, in a number of ways, NAA's proposed NA-21 exceeded requirements. Still, against bomber-producing stalwarts like the aforementioned, NAA's chance for a successful venture was dismal at best. Nevertheless, the vibrant aeronautical engineering staff at NAA was determined to make its proposed NA-21 much more than runners-up.

In late 1935 NAA had moved from Dundalk, Maryland, to the Inglewood and El Segundo area of Los Angeles, California, adjacent to Mines Field (now LAX). Since its move, the company had only produced single-engine observation and basic training aircraft. Nevertheless, NAA initiated engineering work on what it called the "twin-engine bomber." It was 1 April 1936.

Chief Design Engineer John Leland "Lee" Atwood and his assistant Ray-mond H. "Ray" Rice came up with a large, heavy airplane with several unique features—turbosuperchargers, powered machine gun turrets, and fully regulated crew station oxygen outlets for high altitude operation. What is more, it featured accommodations for eight crew members and the ability to carry an extra heavy bomb load within its belly (up to 10,000lb!). The total engineering time on the NA-21, program start to the first release of drawings to the X-shop on 1 October 1936 (drafting hours and other group's hours), was 64,837 hours. The airplane, sporting two turbosupercharged 800hp Pratt & Whitney Aircraft R-1830 Twin Wasp engines, was completed on 22 December 1936 and prepared for flight test.

On New Year's Day 1937, propelled by its pair of air-cooled, two-row radial engines with experimental turbosuperchargers, D. W. "Tommy" Tomlinson, a

civilian and freelance multiengine test pilot, completed a successful first flight of the NA-21 at Mines Field.

Later flights at Wright Army Air Field near Dayton, Ohio, found its propulsion system to be unworthy and the plane was eliminated from further contention in favor of the Douglas DB-1 (Douglas Bomber-One) design, forerunner of the previously mentioned B-18 Bolo. Soon, under a follow-on US-AAC contract, the airplane was ferried back to California for additional research and experimentation.

Confident that its losing NA-21 design had potential, NAA offered the US-AAC a revised version powered instead by two 910hp Pratt & Whitney R-2180 Twin Hornets with the improved F-10 turbosupercharger unit that boosted maximum horsepower—at high altitude—to 1,250hp. Additionally, the air-

plane featured improved armament and more streamlining.

North American's new version, known in-house as model NA-39, was well received. So an amended USAAC contract for the NA-21-cum-NA-39 was approved, and in October 1937 NAA initiated engineering work on the design, now designated XB-21, and unofficially named "Dragon Bomber."

## The XB-21 (NA-39)

The USAAC contract for a single XB-21 airplane had been approved on 14 May 1938, and four months later in September, after 20,666 engineering hours, the first drawings of the NA-39 were released to the X-shop. All in all, it took NAA's mechanics three months to complete the NA-21 to NA-39 transformation processes. And on 22 December, with Tommy Tomlinson at the controls

The XB-21 (NA-39) evolved from the NA-21 to meet a 1935 USAAC requirement but lost out to the Douglas B-18A Bolo, primarily due to per airplane cost. NAA had quoted a unit price of $122,600 for fifty-plane batches whereas Douglas quoted a unit price of $63,977—nearly half as much. *Rockwell*

once again, the XB-21 successfully completed its first flight at Mines Field.

Much improved, the XB-21 was ferried to Wright Field in early 1939. The XB was still guilty of lackluster performance, though, and the USAAC turned it down as well. Undaunted, NAA offered to build five service test YB-21 airplanes and, at a unit price of $122,600, fifty-plane production batches of B-21As.

Douglas Aircraft on the other hand had offered its better-performing B-18

Rare view of the XB-21 as it prepares for its first flight in early 1937 at Mines Field. The "Dragon" bomber was a clean but somewhat portly midwing airplane powered by two Pratt & Whitney R-2180-1 radials rated at 1,250hp for take-off. It was about the same size as Douglas' famed DC-3/C-47 series. *Rockwell*

for a unit price of $63,977—$58,623 less! These differences in performance and monies made it easy for the USAAC to make a quick decision. In April 1939, since the Douglas B-18 was superior in performance and could be procured at nearly half the price, the North American B-21 Dragon was soundly eliminated from further contention. The USAAC had purchased the airplane, however, and therefore retained it for use as a laboratory airplane at Wright Field. It served there for many years as an engine test bed among other things before it was ultimately scrapped; NAA's total engineering time on the XB-21 project came to 22,070 hours.

Earlier on 18 January 1938 the USAAC had issued to the industry CP No. 38-385. This circular proposal called for an advanced twin-engine light-class attack bomber. And again a number of airframe contractors, including NAA, went to work on their respective designs. North American entered the competition with its model NA-40.

## The NA-40

In September 1938, after 105,161 total engineering hours, the first NA-40 drawings were released to the X-shop to initiate construction of one airplane. Since the USAAC had neither ordered nor designated the proposed airplane, NAA and the others were compelled to develop it with their own monies.

Determined to break into the bombardment and attack bombardment aircraft market, NAA again counted on its hard-working engineering staff. On 10 February 1939, some five months after its first metal was cut, the NA-40 was completed and prepared for flight test.

The NA-40 was a twin-engine, three-place, high-wing plane with twin vertical stabilizers. The airplane sported fully retractable tricycle-type landing gear, a relatively new development at the time. One of the interesting features of the NA-40 was its underslung engine nacelles, pioneered by NAA on the XB-21 Dragon. This nacelle position was found to be highly desirable from the standpoint of low drag and high propulsion efficiency, and subsequently adapted for use on most American multiengine, piston-powered, propeller-driven aircraft. To further reduce drag, it also featured a long streamlined cockpit canopy to cover the pilot and copilot seated in tandem under the greenhouse-type enclosure.

Powered by a pair of 1,100hp Pratt & Whitney R-1830 Twin Wasp engines and piloted by NAA test pilot Paul Balfour, the NA-40 made a successful first flight at Mines Field on 3 March 1939. Although its turbosupercharged Twin Wasp radials generated advertised horsepower (up some 300hp from the original R-1830 engines that powered the

NA-21), the performance of the NA-40 was not acceptable.

To increase the performance of the NA-40 attack bomber, NAA opted to replace the engines with relatively new 1,125hp Wright Aeronautical Company R-2600 Cyclone 14s. The Cyclone 14—a fourteen-cylinder, two-row, air-cooled radial engine, with turbosupercharging—was advertised to produce 1,350hp at high altitude. At the time, more important, it allowed the NA-40B (as the NA-40 was redesignated after engine modification) to perform as desired.

In March 1939, the NA-40B was ferried to Wright Army Air Field to participate in the USAAC attack bomber competition.

After two weeks of testing there, with its new uprated R-2600 engines, the modified NA-40B boasted an exceptional 285mph top speed. Had NAA's day finally arrived? Just when it seemed that it had at long last developed a winner, fate stepped in.

Following a flight test on 11 April 1939, USAAC Pilot Maj. Younger Pitts prepared to land NAA's NA-40B. While he entered the approach pattern to Wright Army Air Field, Pitts lost control and the airplane crashed. The one-of-a-kind airplane was destroyed in the fire that ensued. Amazingly, however, the three-man crew escaped the crash without serious injuries. The cause of the crash was later ruled to be pilot error.

The NA-40B's short-lived flight test program demonstrated spectacular performance. But since the USAAC was forced to quickly decide on the winning

Circa 1937 phantom view of the XB-21 illustrates the crew accommodations, proposed tricycle landing gear (it was built as a tail dragger), ball-type nose turret and dorsal turret, bomb bay, and the waist and ventral gun positions. *Rockwell*

Production B-21s would have been able to carry a maximum bomb load of 10,000lb—large for the era. For self-defense, it was to be armed with five .30-caliber machine guns at five different stations. Its maximum speed was 220mph and its cruise speed was 190mph; it was able to climb 1,000ft per minute. *Rockwell*

Red Hansen (right) was XB-21 project engineer and, later, B-25 project engineer. Ed Horkey (second from left) was a key aerodynamicist on the XB-21, NA-40, and B-25. D. W. Tomlinson (between Horkey and Hansen) was the primary XB-21 test pilot; Paul Balfour is at left. *Rockwell*

attack bomber design—for export to France and Great Britain due to darkening war clouds in Europe—there simply was not enough time to build and evaluate another NA-40 attack bomber plane. Instead NAA's strongest rival, the Douglas DB-7 (Douglas Bomber-Seven, which became the A-20 Havoc), was ordered into production. Therefore, after a total of 116,387 engineering hours,

NAA terminated work on its NA-40 in May 1939.

With war looming on the horizon, airframe contractors were afforded little time to respond to USAAC circular proposals. So when NAA responded to CP No. 39-640, which won a contract to build 184 B-25 type airplanes, the atmosphere was electric and work had to be accomplished at lightning speed. Moreover, there would not be time to construct an experimental NA-62 airplane.

## The NA-62

From the outset of the NA-62 program, due to the USAAC's dire need for bombardment type aircraft, no X (experimental) or Y (service test) B-25 type

airplanes were ordered or built. All 184 B-25s would be production airplanes. Though the B-25 was an altogether new airplane, the engineering staff at NAA used to good advantage the extensive experience gained developing the NA-40. Based on the NA-40, the B-25 proposal was prepared in forty days, during which time the engineering design group worked long hours under considerable pressure. The numerous performance calculations necessary were rendered more difficult because, at the time, wind tunnel tests were unavailable.

Approximately 10,000 engineering hours had already been expended on the NA-62 project when the initial contract for 184 B-25 type airplanes was ap-

The immediate forerunner of the B-25 was the proposed light attack bomber—the NA-40, which never received a designation. Shown here in its original roll-out dress, the NA-40 (civil registration number X14221) was one of the first aircraft to feature tricycle landing gear and underslung engine nacelles to lessen aerodynamic drag. Its twin tail configuration was later adopted for the B-25. *Rockwell*

proved on 20 September 1939. In the following months, the engineering hours built up steadily to a peak of almost 39,000 in March 1940—the month before the first drawings were released to the shop. From the release date of 13 April 1940 until February 1941, monthly engineering hours stayed below 30,000. Thereafter, however, maintenance engineering on the first contract combined with development engineering on subsequent models forced engineering activity to escalate steadily.

When word was received that the NA-62 design had been accepted, NAA immediately began work on a one-ninth scale model of the B-25 for use in wind-tunnel tests. These tests were conducted in the wind tunnel at the California Institute of Technology as soon as the model was finished; it greatly accelerated the design development.

The full-scale wood mockup of the B-25 type bomber—complete with instruments, seats, and controls—was started at the same time that work began on the scale wind-tunnel model. The USAAC Mockup Board visited NAA's Inglewood plant on 9 November 1939 and, with minor changes, approved the design. The time had finally

come and NAA prepared for efficient quantity production.

## Efficient Quantity Production

In light of the B-25's production requirements, one of the most significant aspects of its initial development was the design breakdown of the airframe for efficient quantity production. Until NAA applied the component breakdown method of design and manufacture to its aircraft, the style used in assembling aircraft was pretty much the same as in the days of the Wright Brothers. This method consisted essentially of assembling the fuselage skeleton in a large jig or cradle; then installing in the fuselage the various cables, lines, brackets, and other equipment; and finally building on the wings, tail group, and other assemblies necessary to make a complete airplane.

The original component breakdown of the B-25 bomber, which provided for about forty-eight major component sections, was trend-setting and is still used today.

The original design of the B-25 medium-class bomber provided for a midwing airplane powered by two 1,650hp Wright R-2600-9 Cyclone 14 engines, spinning

Hamilton Standard, hydromatic, three-bladed propellers. Provisions were made for a crew of five, which included pilot, copilot, bombardier, navigator/radio operator, and gunner. The bomb load was calculated at more than 2,000lb, and a speed of over 300mph was guaranteed.

Armament on the first B-25 consisted of a flexible .30cal machine gun in the nose of the bombardier's compartment, capable of being used in three positions; one flexible .30cal machine gun mounted in the upper rear fuselage; and one flexible .30cal machine gun in the rear fuselage called a waist gun with firing positions on either side of the rear fuselage and in the floor. In the tail was a flexible .50cal machine gun operated by a gunne rseated inside a clam shell-type enclosure. There was no armor

A 1939 artist concept view of the proposed NA-62 prior to the first production contract for 184 B-25 type airplanes; drawn by NAA's Al Algier. *Rockwell*

plate in the airplane, and the fuel tanks were not self-sealing.

## Procurement Policy

In addition to being one of the largest contracts ever placed by the US-AAC to date, the initial B-25 contract of 20 September 1939 marked a new departure in USAAC procurement policy. Previously, airframe contractors had been required to build experimental (or prototype) models, and to wait for a production contract until a year or more of intensive testing had been completed on the experimental airplane. Since pro-

duction preparations following the placement of the production contract often required as long as two or three years, it was not unusual for a period of five years to elapse between the start of design work and the first production deliveries to the services. Under the new procurement policy, dictated by the growing national emergency, the US-AAC placed a production contract for "paper airplanes." That is, for airplanes that only existed in certain design drawings and performance estimates submitted by the manufacturer. The B-25 contract was one of the first of these "paper airplane" contracts, whereby the untried airplane was essentially flown off the drawing boards. But it proved effective.

Proof of the new policy's effectiveness may be found in the fact that pro-

duction deliveries were underway just seventeen months after production engineering had started in September 1939. At the time of Pearl Harbor, the USAAC had received delivery on 130 of the 184 airplanes provided for in the contract, whereas under previous procurement policies it is reasonable to assume that only the barest beginnings of preparations for production would have been achieved in that time period (witness today's B-2 production program).

In this light it may be noted that any procurement policy may have failed to quickly build an adequate air force without skilled industrial organizations large enough to serve as nuclei for the badly needed expansion.

In the instance of the B-25 program, at the time the program started NAA had approximately 3,700 employees, all with previous military aircraft experience. Although the rapid expansion of the NAA organization (it had almost doubled a year later and more than quadrupled two years later) was no less difficult than might be expected, it is obvious that the task would have been virtually impossible if the starting nucleus had not already existed. Editorially speaking, this conveys a lesson for the future: America's security requires experienced organizations able to design and produce quickly in a national emergency.

## Winning Designs

After the USAAC approved NAA's NA-62 and Martin's M-179, it asked for financial bids, and on 10 August 1939, letters of intent were announced for the two winning designs.

Although bearing very different twin-engine medium-class bombardment aircraft designs, both North American and Martin met the challenge. Respectively, cost per unit was quoted at $7,868.15 and $6,397.28 for a difference in price of $1,470.87. This difference in price, it can be assumed, dictated the difference in ordered units—that is, 184 B-25s versus 201 B-26s.

In its procurement of two untried aircraft, of course, the USAAC had taken quite a chance. Ultimately, each type found success.

Martin elected to power its B-26 type with the new and unproved 1,850 hp turbosupercharged Pratt & Whitney R-2800 Double Wasp engine. North American had opted to power its B-25 type with the proved 1,650hp turbosupercharged Wright R-2600 Cyclone 14 engine. Both engine types featured growth potential, but as they developed, the Double Wasp clearly outclassed the Cyclone.

Nevertheless, with a contract in hand for 184 B-25 type airplanes, NAA's young and brilliant engineering staff went to work on three design versions of model NA-62. As ordered, NAA was to build twenty-four B-25s (NA-62), forty B-25As (NA-62A), and 120 B-25Bs (NA-62B). Though minor in nature, these differences were significant to the ultimate success of what became a classic

B-25 Project engineer Red Hansen (right) and others look on during a wind-tunnel test at the California Institute of Technology. *Rockwell*

twin-engine medium-class bombardment airplane—the B-25.

## XB-21 "Dragon" Specifications

| | |
|---|---|
| Type | Eight-place, twin-engine, light-to-medium-class bomber |
| Wingspan | 95ft, 0in |
| Wing area | 1,120sq-ft |
| Length | 61ft, 9in |
| Height | 14ft, 9in |
| Empty weight | 19,082lb |
| Maximum weight | 40,000lb |
| Maximum speed | 220mph @ 10,000ft |
| Maximum range | 1,960mi with 2,400gal fuel and 2,200lb bomb load; 660mi with 10,000lb bomb load |
| Service ceiling | 25,000ft |
| Climb rate | 1,000fpm |
| Armament | Five flexible .30cal machine guns: one in nose turret, one in tail turret, one in top turret, and one waist gun on either side of the fuselage |
| Powerplant | Two twin-row, air-cooled turbosupercharged Pratt & Whitney R-2180 Twin Hornet 1,250hp radial engines (910hp normal) |

## NA-40B Specifications

| | |
|---|---|
| Type | Five-place, twin-engine, light-class attack bomber |
| Wingspan | 66ft, 0in |
| Wing area | 599sq-ft |
| Length | 47ft, 10in |
| Height | 15ft, 0in |
| Empty weight | 12,350lb |
| Maximum weight | 20,000lb |
| Maximum speed | 287mph @ 5,000ft |
| Maximum range | 1,180mi with 1,200lb bomb load |
| Service ceiling | 25,000ft |
| Climb rate | 1,450fpm |
| Armament | Three flexible .30cal machine guns: one in ball-type nose turret, one in top turret, and one for either the ventral turret or either waist position |
| Powerplant | Two twin-row, air-cooled turbosupercharged Wright R-2600 Cyclone 14 1,600hp radial engines (1,100hp normal) |

*Chapter 2*

# Reincarnation

To design, develop, and build a successful twin-engine medium-class bomber, NAA's respected president Dutch Kindleberger relied heavily on the expertise of his outstanding engineering staff—especially NAA vice president and assistant general manager Lee Atwood. In turn, Atwood was confident of his assistant and NAA chief engineer Ray Rice. And Rice depended on preliminary design engineer Edgar Schmued, structural engineer Richard L. "Dick" Schleicher, aerodynamicist Edward J. "Ed" Horkey, and project engineer Walter A. "Walt" Spivak, who replaced Red Hansen when he moved up in the organization. Many other key players, of course, greatly contributed to the immense success of the B-25 program.

Since the USAAC had approved and ordered NAA's design of the B-25 type airplane, its final configuration (with minor changes to be discussed later) was solidified on 12 August 1939. Simultaneously, NAA management authorized the start of construction processes on twenty-five airframes—one for static structural strength evaluations, and twenty-four flyable B-25 type airplanes. Gutted internally, the static test airframe was completed first and then

A ground crewman checks for the proper action of the cowl flaps on the number one engine on the first B-25 just before its premiere flight. *Rockwell*

shipped to Wright Field on Independence Day 1940.

Meanwhile, without having established a full-scale B-25 production line as yet, construction work proceeded within a cordoned-off area of the Inglewood plant. As the first flyable B-25 type airplane neared completion in late July 1940, work continued on the next two examples.

As it was designed and built, the B-25 fuselage had an all-metal semi-monocoque airframe structure of 24 ST aluminum alloy (monocoque meaning that all or most of the airframe stresses are carried by the skin of the airplane), divided into three major sections: the forward section to include the bombardier/nose gunner station, the pilot/copilot compartment, and the navigator area; the intermediate section to include the bomb bay and passageway above it; and the rear section to include the radio operator/waist gunner area, the camera station, and the tail gunner compartment.

The forward fuselage section includes the area from the nose of the airplane to the bulkhead that forms the forward end of the bomb bay. The bombardier/nose gunner station is in the nose of the forward fuselage section and is entered through a passageway under the left side of the pilot/copilot compartment. The station contains a riding seat for the bombardier/nose gunner, a mount for the bomb sight, the bomb

rack control panels, fixed or flexible .30cal or .50cal machine guns, and ammunition. The upper half of the transparent nose section (except later solid-nose types) is bolted to the lower solid half, which is stressed skin structure with aluminum floor panels. The left-hand side of the bombardier/nose gunner station has an emergency escape hatch.

Aft of the bombardier/nose gunner station is the pilot/copilot compartment, which is enclosed by the fuselage skin and transparent cockpit window panels. The floor is of aluminum panels, and an emergency escape hatch is located directly above the seats of the pilot and copilot. The navigator area is directly behind the pilot/copilot station. The upper gun turret compartment (on later versions) is also directly behind the pilot/copilot station. The navigator/upper gun turret compartment contains the command receiver and the radio compass receiver. And the forward fuselage entrance hatch is located just aft of the nose landing gear well.

The intermediate fuselage section includes the bomb bay and the passageway from the navigator/upper gun turret area to the waist gunner/lower gun turret station. The sides of the bomb bay are formed by the fuselage skin, and the top is formed by the floor of the passageway; a covered manhole in the center of the passageway provides access to the bomb bay. The bottom of the bomb

The first three B-25 airplanes (the number one B-25 is in the foreground) nearing completion in "the shop" at NAA's Inglewood plant, circa July 1940. Note the unbroken dihedral wings. *Rockwell*

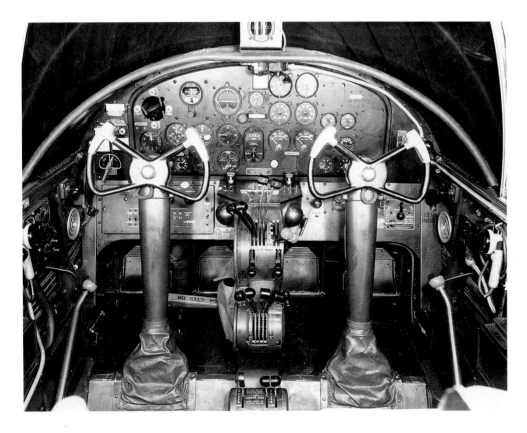

A view of the pilot and copilot stations in B-25 number one illustrate just how sparse and "old fashioned" aircraft cockpits were in the early 1940s. *Rockwell*

bay is closed off by the outward-opening/inward-closing bomb bay doors mounted ventrally on centerline.

The rear fuselage section extends aftward of the bomb bay to the end of the fuselage. Entrance to this section is through the rear entrance hatch or through the passageway over the bomb bay. The forward part of the rear fuselage section forms the waist gunner, lower gun turret, camera, radio, and tail gunner compartments. An escape hatch, which can be opened from either inside or outside the airplane, is located immediately aft of the waist gunner/lower gun turret areas.

The B-25 wing is a full cantilever structure (cantilever meaning there are no external support struts or bracing), consisting of a center section integral with the intermediate fuselage section and two outer wing panels. The wing structure is made of aluminum alloy extrusions, spars, and power-pressed ribs covered by Alclad sheet metal. The wing center section supports the engine nacelles and main landing gear. Fuel tank compartments incorporated in the center section structure house self-sealing fuel tanks (non-self-sealing at first). The outer wing panels are bolted to the wing center section. Metal-framed, metal-covered wing tips are attached to the outer wing panels by screws through the skin of the outer wing panels. Hydraulically operated, all-metal, trailing-edge wing flaps of the slotted type extend from either side of the fuselage to the engine nacelles, and from the nacelles to the inboard end of each aileron. Metal-framed, fabric-covered ailerons are installed on each outer wing panel; counterweights balance the ailerons statically.

The fixed empennage (tail group) structure consists of a metal-covered horizontal stabilizer with a metal-covered vertical stabilizer attached to each tip. Metal-framed, fabric-covered elevators and rudders are hinged to the horizontal and vertical stabilizers. The horizontal stabilizer is attached to the upper rear fuselage section by means of bolted fittings that join the front and rear stabilizer spars to the fuselage. Each vertical stabilizer is an all-metal structure bolted to the front and rear spars of the horizontal stabilizer. The vertical stabilizers extend both above and below the horizontal stabilizer. The structure of ribs, spars, and light rolled stringers is

covered by 24 ST aluminum skin. Detachable tips provide access to the interior structure of the vertical stabilizers. All-metal trim tabs are attached to the elevators and rudders by three sealed ball-bearing hinges. A horn protruding from the side of the tab at the center hinge provides means of attaching the tab actuating rod.

The flying surfaces consist of rudders, elevators, ailerons, and flaps. The rudders, elevators, and ailerons are conventionally controlled by duplicate control cable systems; each system is designed so that the loss of any one control cable through gunfire would not seriously cripple the airplane. The wing flaps are normally operated by hydraulically actuated struts; however, an emer-

gency mechanical operating system has been incorporated in the wing flap control system.

The B-25 employed a hydraulically operated tricycle type landing gear system, which was the relatively new replacement for the "tail dragger" type. An emergency hydraulic system, independent of the normal hydraulic system, is used for emergency extension and down-lock of the landing gear. All three landing gear assemblies retract aftward—that is, each main gear assembly into its respective engine nacelle bay, and the nose gear assembly into its bay in the forward section of the fuselage. Fairing doors cover the landing gear bays when the gear is either extended or retracted, except where the assemblies

The number one B-25 being prepared for an early flight-test at Mines Field. Though very different than its earlier predecessor, the plane's overall appearance is reminiscent of the NA-40B. *Rockwell*

protrude downward from their respective attachment points. A position indicator, which indicates the position and the locked/unlocked condition of the three landing gear assemblies, is located on the cockpit instrument panel.

The B-25's hydraulic system operates not only the landing gear but also the wing flaps, brakes, engine cowl flaps, and the bomb bay doors. The engine cowl flaps have separate control handles for the left and the right en-

Shown in civilian attire in front of the number one B-25 are General Knudsen (left), General Arnold (center), and James Kindelberger—respectively, Chief of the Office of Procurement Management for the USAAC, Chief of the USAAC, and President of North American Aviation, Inc. Shortly after this photograph was taken, they witnessed the premier B-25 make its first flight on 19 August 1940. *Associated Press via Rockwell*

gines, and the operation of the cowl flaps or wing flaps may be stopped at any desired position by returning the control handles to neutral. The landing gear emergency lowering and downlock system is supplied by a separate hand-pump and reservoir.

The B-25 has an independent fuel system for each engine. The main fuel supply is four large self-sealing wing tanks (non-self-sealing at first), two located in each wing center section between the fuselage and engine nacelles. The front and rear main tanks on each side are connected by a line that extends from the rear tank to an adapter,

mounted on the front tank, to which an electrically operated booster pump is attached. A check valve in the adapter permits fuel to flow from the rear tank to the front tank and then to the engine, but prevents the fuel from returning to the rear tank. From the booster pump fuel flows to a strainer mounted on the firewall and then to the engine-driven pump, which delivers the fuel to the carburetor. An auxiliary fuel supply, consisting of six smaller self-sealing tanks installed in groups of three in each wing center section outboard of the main fuel tanks, is also provided. The front main and the three outboard tanks in each group are interconnected with the rear main by a line extending from each tank aft through the nacelle to an electrically operated transfer pump mounted to the aft auxiliary tank access door.

For extended range requirements, both droppable and nondroppable tanks could be installed in the bomb bay beneath the upper main tanks. These tanks, when installed, interconnected with the main fuel tanks. Also,

provisions were made for the installation of additional auxiliary fuel tanks (one under either outer wing panel) for long-range ferrying activities.

As mentioned earlier, the first North American B-25 bomber was completed on 6 August 1940. Gleaming in a natural aluminum alloy finish, it sported the USAAC markings of the day. On the outside of each vertical tail were seven red and six white horizontal stripes with a blue vertical bar alongside the stripes. "US Army" was stenciled in black beneath the wings ("US" below the right wing and "Army" below the left wing); and it had four blue roundels with red dots centered in white stars—two above and two below each wing tip. Its completion was immediately followed with engine run-ups and other ground-based check-outs of its hydraulic, electrical, and fuel systems. Then, with NAA test pilot Vance Breese at the controls, low- and medium-speed taxi tests began. These checked the brakes, nose wheel steering, rudder effectiveness, and so on.

During one of the early taxi tests the nose landing gear structure collapsed

With Vance Breese (pilot) and Roy Ferren (flight-test engineer) under glass, the first of 9,889 Mitchell bombers heads toward the Pacific Ocean during its premier flight. The airplane—sleek even by today's standards—displays its original vertical tails, engine exhaust stacks (pipes), and unbroken dihedral wings. *Rockwell*

The B-25 featured a tricycle landing gear configuration that was a relatively new advancement in landing gear technology when it appeared. This type of landing gear ultimately did away with the earlier "tail dragger" arrangement (witness the XB-21 in chapter one). *Rockwell*

Head-on view of an early B-25 illustrates the unbroken dihedral wing used on the first nine B-25 airplanes. This particular wing planform, coupled with inadequate area on the vertical stabilizers, contributed to the B-25's early Dutch roll problem. *Rockwell*

The B-25's wide-stance main landing gear offered stable ground handling during taxiing, take-off runs, and landing roll-outs. The pear-shaped vertical stabilizers shown here were abandoned in favor of larger area tails. *Rockwell*

and the airplane nose-dived into the runway. The nose landing gear wheel shimmy damper broke and excess wheel shimmy was blamed for the collapse of the nose gear. Following the repair of its nose landing gear, and after additional low- and medium-speed taxi tests, the new airplane was cleared for its maiden flight. It had only been eleven months since contract approval and, amazingly, the first B-25 was about to enter into its specialized environment—the sky.

Then on 19 August 1940, sounding like twenty-eight raging cyclones and shining like a newly minted silver dollar, one very good-looking airplane ran up its two R-2600 engines just before its first takeoff and flight. With pilot Vance Breese in the left-hand seat and flight test engineer Roy Ferren in the right-hand seat, the new B-25 rotated, lifted off, and climbed up and away from the runway at Mines Field on its flight test out over the Pacific Ocean. After several flights, Breese talked of his satisfaction with the airplane. On the other hand, NAA flight test engineer Ferren reported

unacceptable rolling and yawing problems. Nevertheless, flight test activities continued.

During subsequent flight evaluations of the first B-25 and others, a number of vertical tail and rudder configurations were evaluated to correct the aircraft's roll and yaw characteristics. Finally, after some four different sizes and shapes were tested, those serious aerodynamic problems were eliminated (see below).

As a matter of interest, with Martin test pilot William K. "Ken" Ebel at the controls, the premier Martin B-26—to be named Marauder—made its first flight out of Martin's Baltimore, Maryland, facility on 25 November 1940. The aircraft suffered from high wing loading and crashes became commonplace; the problem was later cured and full-scale production ensued.

In addition to the single static test airframe, the USAAC had ordered twenty-four production B-25 (NA-62) airplanes under contract number AC-13258, which was approved by Secretary of War Henry L. Stimson on 20 September 1939 through the Departments of War.

On 22 November 1940—three months after the first B-25 had made its maiden flight—the USAAC 689 Engineering Board inspected the B-25 and

found no serious flaws from an engineering standpoint.

When first ordered, oddly, the first B-25s (including the B-25As and B-25Bs to be discussed below) had the prefix "R" for Restricted, which indicated that these aircraft were not for use on combat missions! But when the first B-25s began to roll out of NAA's Inglewood plant in late 1940, war was already raging in Europe and the "R" prefix was eliminated. For a short time, however, the aircraft were designated RB-25, RB-25A, and RB-25B. Obviously then, since the war had begun, all B-25s were immediately cleared for use on combat missions. The first five airplanes were accepted in February 1941, with nine additional aircraft the following month.

As flight test evaluations continued on the first B-25, USAAC Capt. Frank Cook—a test pilot from Wright Field who had been assigned to investigate the B-25's stability and control qualities (he also did this on the B-26 flight test program)—noticed a Dutch roll condition that, with the intended use of the super-secret Norden bomb sight, would not allow the B-25 to be a stable enough bombardment platform. Dutch roll on aircraft is a lateral (side-to-side along the wingspan) oscillation with a pronounced rolling (wing tip up/wing tip down) motion. After a series of wind-tunnel inves-

tigations, two major aerodynamic flaws were discovered: first, the constant anhedral (negative dihedral) of the wing; and second the relatively small area of the vertical stabilizers.

To correct the problem—Dutch roll—NAA aerodynamicists suggested that the B-25's outer wing panels, from the engine nacelles outward, have zero dihedral. Thus, the B-25's unmistakable bent-wings (or gull-wings) were employed to create negative dihedral on the aircraft's inboard wing panels and zero dihedral on the outboard wing panels (the dihedral angle on an aircraft's wing improves lateral stability).

To cure the second problem, NAA

aerodynamicists advised using larger vertical stabilizers. And as mentioned above, after some four shapes and sizes were tested in-flight, the final vertical stabilizer area was discovered and applied.

These fixes worked for the most part, and as a result, the B-25 became an accurate bombing platform. In fact, a number of bombardment groups that used the B-25 during World War II enjoyed citations for their bombardment accurateness.

As has been reported in other references on the B-25 (albeit undocumented), the first nine airplanes off the assembly line had unbroken dihedral

The number ten B-25 with the first broken dihedral wing installation completed on 18 April 1941. The window on top of the fuselage is noteworthy. *Rockwell*

wings; from B-25 number ten and on, the broken dihedral wings were common to the plane. It remains unclear as to whether the first nine B-25s were all retroactively fitted with broken dihedral wings. At least two, number one and number four, were retrofitted, however.

NAA, for its own purposes, kept the number one B-25 airplane, serial number 40-2165 (see chapter eight). The re-

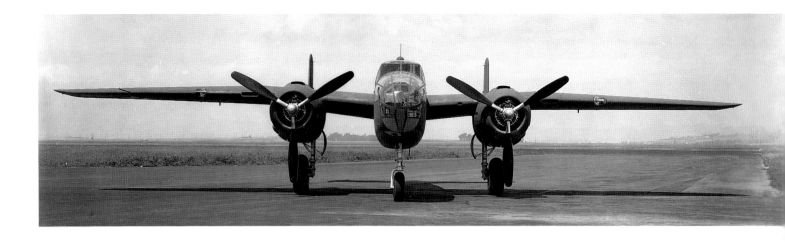

Head-on view of a B-25 with the new broken dihedral wing made the type appear to have a gull-wing. Chance Vought's F4U Corsair, a naval fighter plane, likewise had a gull-wing that earned it the nickname of the "bent-wing bird." Also note the B-25's upturned wing tips, which helped its stalling characteristics and allowed relatively short take-offs and landings. *Rockwell*

mainder of the first production batch of twenty-four B-25s was accepted by the USAAC-cum-USAAF. Out of those twenty-three aircraft, nineteen went to Mc-Chord AAF, two went to Wright AAF, one went to Chanute AAF, and one went to Lowry AAF.

While those four that went to Wright, Chanute, and Lowry were used for ongoing flight test and evaluation purposes, the nineteen that went to Mc-Chord just south of Tacoma, Washington, were first used for coastal defense with the 17th Bombardment Group.

The number four B-25 (40-2168) was returned to NAA in mid-1943 to undergo modification to become a personal transport for USAAF commander Hap Arnold (see chapter eight); the USAAF was established on 20 June 1941, and the USAAC was at the same time disestablished.

Earlier on 25 February 1941, after NAA had installed the modified gull-wing on the number ten B-25 (40-2174),

Two "Rosies the Riveters" install wire bundles in the forward fuselage section (looking forward) of a B-25. Indeed, as this photograph shows, miles and miles of electrical wiring are used in the construction of aircraft. And the one shown was built some fifty years ago. *Rockwell*

In-flight view of an early B-25A shows the configuration of the vertical stabilizers that never again changed. With its relatively high aspect ratio, the B-25's wing did not have high wing-loading like Martin's B-26. *Rockwell*

It was flight tested at Mines Field for about two hours. North American chief test pilot Edward W. "Ed" Virgin and his copilot, NAA test pilot Louis S. Wait, agreed after this flight that the B-25's Dutch roll problem was now eliminated. The wing modification brought aerodynamic perfection, and the basic design of the wing was never again altered.

After Virgin and Wait had flown the revised B-25 with the broken dihedral wing, Maj. Donald Stace—in charge of US Army aircraft acceptances at NAA's Inglewood plant—took it up on a one-hour test hop. He also agreed that the modified wing had indeed cured the Dutch roll problem.

## Rebirth

NAA vice president and general manager Lee Atwood coined what would become the B-25's official name—Mitchell, in honor of the late Maj. Gen. William S. "Billy" Mitchell. The famed Billy Mitchell, regarded by most as one of America's key architects

A portrait of Maj. Gen. William S. "Billy" Mitchell by an unknown artist. *Rockwell*

of air power, a "prophet who died without honor," was the assistant chief of the US Army Air Service from 1919 to 1925 when he was unjustly court-martialed for his attempts to sell the importance of the airplane as a bombing platform to the military establishment. Mitchell's proposition was met with laughter and contempt. Following his court-martial, he was stripped of his command and reduced in rank from Brigadier General to Colonel. Worse, since he was a master tactician and excellent flyer, he was grounded and placed behind a desk. Billy Mitchell died prematurely at the age of fifty-seven on 19 February 1936. Ironically, he died at the very same time his prophecies were beginning to be realized. After his untimely death, Mitchell was posthumously reinstated as a general officer, to the higher rank of Major General.

One of Mitchell's advocates, NAA's Lee Atwood, said, "Very early in the [B-25] project several of us were having a bull session in [Dutch] Kindleberger's office and the subject of a name for the new bomber was brought up. I suggested that it be named after General Billy Mitchell but nothing was decided at that time. In a later conversation we settled on Mitchell." When the B-25 was officially named Mitchell, in essence Billy Mitchell was reborn in another body.

## The B-25A (NA-62A)

In addition to twenty-four B-25s, the USAAC ordered forty B-25A (NA-62A) airplanes. This type was the first true production version of the Mitchell bomber plane. In addition to its new configuration—broken dihedral wings, vertical stabilizers, and so on—the B-25A featured armored areas for crew protection and self-sealing fuel tanks.

An intent aerodynamicist contemplates the size and volume of the B-25's bomb bay area where it could carry a large torpedo. Many such wind tunnel evaluations were carried out to determine different weapons-carrying capabilities of the Mitchell bombers. *Rockwell*

This close-up in-flight view of a B-25A illustrates its final aerodynamic configuration—that is, straight outboard wing panels and the larger area vertical stabilizers and rudders. *Rockwell*

Now featuring upper and lower machine gun turrets, and no tail turret, the first B-25B airplane posed during a photo opportunity at Inglewood. *Rockwell*

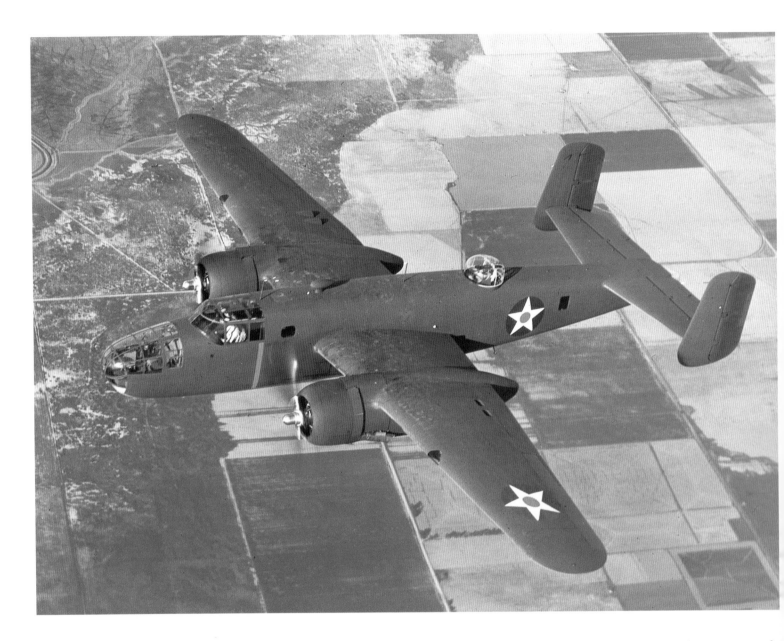

In glorious color, the number one B-25B shows off its lines during an early test hop over Southern California. It was this model that the Doolittle Raiders would soon use to enrage the Japanese and renew American pride. *Rockwell*

The changes between the B-25A and the no-suffix B-25 spelled an increase in weight and a reduction in fuel capacity. But crew accommodation and armament remained the same. Although range and performance had decreased, the B-25A Mitchell could still carry a 3,000lb bomb load some 1,350 miles at a top speed of 315mph.

Of the forty B-25As built, six went to the 44th Bombardment Group (BG) at McDill AAF; six went to the 39th BG at Felts AAF; six went to the 30th BG at Esler AAF; six went to the 43rd BG at Bangor, Maine; one went to Wright AAF where it stayed until a B-25B became available; and the remaining fifteen B-25As went to the 17th BG at McChord AAF.

## The B-25B (NA-62B)

In addition to the forty B-25As, the USAAC ordered 120 B-25B airplanes. One B-25B happened to crash before it was accepted and, therefore, the USAAC took delivery of 119 B-25Bs.

Retaining the improvements of its B-25 and B-25A relatives, the B-25B's performance was further decreased because it was produced with dorsal (upper) and ventral (lower) turrets that housed two .50cal machine guns each. To help eliminate unwanted drag, the ventral gun turret was retractable. Though a nice feature, it caused a number of problems for its gunners and was finally eliminated on the B-25H (to be discussed later). The reduced speed, altitude, and range of the B-25B due to the dorsal and ventral turrets was offset somewhat with the elimination of the tail turret. The new upper and lower turrets were to make up for the loss of the tail turret. Like the B-25s and B-25As, the B-25B was powered with the Wright R-2600-9 engine spinning 12ft, 6in diameter three-bladed Hamilton Standard hydromatic propellers.

An unknown number of B-25B type aircraft went to the US Navy and were

USAAC crews prepare to depart Inglewood for McChord AAF and many other airfields around the country, circa mid-1941. At this point in time, they did not know just how important these aircraft would become to the war effort. *Rockwell*

NAA workers prepare brand-new B-25Bs for delivery to the USAAC and its allies. Different national insignias representing the United States, Great Britain, and the Netherlands are shown. The aircraft have just been painted, and the workers remove, among other things, their masking. *Rockwell*

The one-of-a-kind XB-28 (NA-63) is shown shortly after it was completed. Originally conceived as a high-altitude version of the B-25, the XB-28 appeared as a totally different airplane. *Rockwell*

designated as PBJ-1 (P-Patrol, B-Bomber, J-North American, 1-first type). These were used as land-based patrol bombers by the US Marine Corps, primarily, to hunt and kill submarines (see chapter seven).

England's Royal Air Force (RAF) received twenty-three lend-lease B-25Bs. These were known as the Mitchell I aircraft. Russia got two B-25Bs, and the US-AAF got the rest. Of those, Wright AAF got three, Patterson AAF got another three; these were used as service test aircraft. The last of the 119 B-25Bs was accepted in May 1942.

All in all, NAA's engineering hours on the B-25/-25A/-25B totaled 663,887 through January 1943.

## Powerplant System

With one exception (refer to the one-of-a-kind NA-98X airplane in chapter three), the piston-powered propeller-driven B-25 is powered by two Wright Aeronautical Company R-2600 engines.

Called the Cyclone 14 due to its four-teen-cylinder arrangement—in two rows of seven staggered piston cylinders—the R-2600 is an air-cooled radial engine that develops up to 1,900 takeoff horsepower at 2,000 revolutions per minute (rpm) at sea-level. First used by the USAAC in 1938, the R-2600 Cyclone 14 was an advanced version of Wright's earlier single-row series of Cyclone engines. The B-25 used four versions of the Cyclone 14. These included the R-2600-9, R-2600-13, R-2600-20, and the R-2600-29. Respectively, their power ratings are as follows: the -9, 1,500hp at 2,400rpm; the -13, 1,500hp at 2,400rpm; the -20, 1,600hp at 2,400rpm; and the 29, 1,500hp at 2,800rpm.

For the B-25 program, from mid-1940 to late 1945, the Wright Aeronautical Company produced more than 47,400 R-2600 engines. Considering that 9,889 B-25s came off NAA assembly lines during that era, nearly three spare engines were manufactured for each B-25; 4.79 engines per airplane.

Spinning three-bladed Hamilton Standard hydromatic, full-feathering propellers with diameters of either 12ft and 6in or 12ft and 7in and pitch settings of 23 degrees (low) to 90 degrees (high), the Wright R-2600 Cyclone 14 engine displaces 2,600ci (thus the designation R-2600); the engine has a bore of 6.125in and a stroke of 6.132in. The weights of the four engines used, depending on which dash number, varies between 1,987lb to 2,045lb. Carbureted and turbosupercharged, the Cyclone 14's compression ratio is about seven to one. With an overall length of 6ft and 4in, the R-2600 used by the B-25 airplane employed a number of different engine exhaust stack (pipe) arrangements to help suppress exhaust flames during nighttime missions. These ranged from large-diameter short and long exhausts on early B-25s to small-diameter finger-type Clayton S exhausts on late B-25s.

The Wright R-2600 engines used by the B-25 airplanes came equipped with two-speed turbosuperchargers with a low blower ratio of seven to one (7.06:1 actual) and a high blower ratio of ten to one (10.06:1 actual). Bendix carburetors were used on the B-25, B-25A, and B-25B; however, from the B-25C and on, more reliable Holley carburetors became standard. Air for cooling the engines enters through the engine cowling just aft of the propellers.

The XB-28A (NA-67) during an engine run-up at Inglewood. This second version of the type would have closely compared to the production B-28 (NA-89) airplane that was canceled in early 1943. *Rockwell*

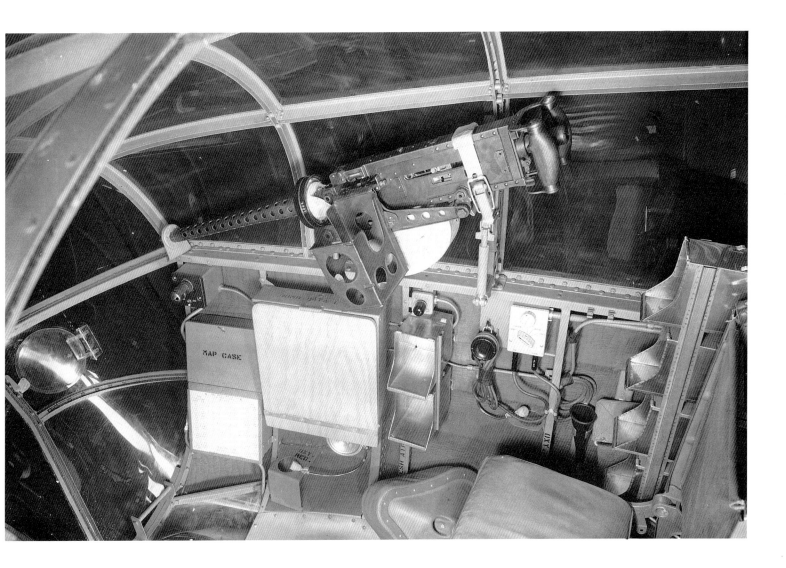

A flexible .30cal machine gun (in the stored position) in the glass nose of a B-25A. Bombardier's and nose gunner's oxygen tube and microphone (lower right near seat) are of interest. *Rockwell*

An exceptionally rare view of the original tail-mounted flexible .50cal machine gun position. An employee of NAA demonstrated how the tail gunner would sit, sight, and fire the gun through the clamshell doors. The hatch above his head was for emergency bail-out in the air, or egress on the ground. *Rockwell*

## High-Altitude Version of the B-25

Earlier, under contract number AC-13583, the USAAC ordered one high-altitude version of the B-25 with fully pressurized crew accommodations. Designated XB-28 (40-3056), engineering on this airplane, which NAA called the "Experimental Bomber," began on 31 August 1939; it was ordered on 13 February 1940.

The proposed high-altitude version of the B-25 would use the turbosupercharged 2,000-plus horsepower Pratt & Whitney R-2800-11 Double Wasp engine for its powerplant system. Not yet a proved engine, NAA's engine choice for the XB-28 airplane was risky business. But the XB-28's projected gross weight of 37,200lb required as much power as possible; thus, the R-2800. As it happened, the B-25's Wright R-2600 engines never reached the horsepower levels of the R-2800. After 415,551 total engineering hours, the first drawings for XB-28 construction were released to the Inglewood factory shop in December 1941 and the first metal was cut.

Except for its circular cross-section fuselage (the standard for fully pressurized aircraft fuselages) to accommodate its five-man crew, the XB-28 closely resembled the B-25. As it developed, though, it became a totally different airplane.

Completed and rolled-out, the XB-28 was initially flight tested at Mines Field on 24 April 1942 by NAA test pilot Ed Virgin.

To create an improved version of the XB-28, under contract number AC-14012, the USAAC ordered one XB-28A airplane. And on 11 November 1939,

NAA initiated engineering on the XB-28A (40-3058). At the same time under a tentative contract for a production version—the B-28—NAA began engineering on NAA model NA-89. Again at Mines Field, the improved XB-28A airplane made its first flight on 17 April 1943.

But, by the time the improved XB-28A had flown, the need for a high-altitude version of the B-25 had been eliminated with the advent of four-engined aircraft like the Boeing B-17 Flying Fortress, Consolidated B-24 Liberator, and Boeing B-29 Superfortress. Therefore, no production contract for the B-28 was forthcoming and the NA-89 program was terminated in January 1943 after only 7,500 total engineering hours.

By this time, however, it really did not matter because more and more B-

25s were being procured. North American had finally produced a winning twin-engine bomber, and was producing it at all-out speed. In fact, to keep up, it had to build another factory at Fairfax Airport in Kansas City, Kansas; construction began on 8 March 1941.

## B-25 Specifications

| | |
|---|---|
| Model number | NA-62 |
| Number built | 24 and one static |
| Type | Five-place, medium-class, twin-engine bombardment airplane |
| Wingspan | 67ft, 6in |
| Wing area | 610sq-ft |
| Length | 54ft, 1in |
| Height | 14ft, 10in |
| Empty weight | 16,767lb |
| Maximum weight | 27,310lb |
| Maximum speed | 322mph@15,000ft |

A Bendix-built top turret, equipped with two .50cal machine guns, is clearly illustrated in this photograph of a B-25B. Flat-plate gun sight between the gun barrels is noteworthy. *Rockwell*

| | |
|---|---|
| Maximum range | 2,000mi with 916gal fuel and 3,000lb bomb load |
| Service ceiling | 30,000ft |
| Climb rate | 2,090fpm |
| Armament | One flexible .50cal machine gun in the tail; three flexible .30cal machine guns (nose, waist, and floor) |
| Powerplant | Two fourteen-cylinder, twin-row, air-cooled turbo super charged Wright R-2600-9 Cyclone 14 1,700hp (takeoff) radial engines |
| First flight | 19 August 1940; pilot, Vance Breese |

The lower turret is shown in its fully extended position. Produced by Bendix, these twin-fifty-equipped gun turrets were extremely difficult to man and operate. When they were removed from later versions of the Mitchell, would-be lower gun turret operators rejoiced. *Rockwell*

## B-25A Specifications

| | |
|---|---|
| Model number | NA-62A |
| Number built | 40 |
| Type | Five-place, medium-class, twin-engine bombardment airplane |
| Wingspan | 67ft, 7in |
| Wing area | 610sq-ft |
| Length | 54ft, 1in |
| Height | 15ft, 9in |
| Empty weight | 17,870lb |
| Maximum weight | 27,100lb |
| Maximum speed | 315mph@15,000ft |
| Maximum range | 1,350mi with 916gal fuel and 3,000lb bomb load |
| Service ceiling | 27,000ft |
| Climb rate | 2,785fpm |
| Armament | One flexible .50cal machine gun in the tail; three flexible .30cal machine guns (nose, waist, and floor) |
| Powerplant | Two fourteen-cylinder, twin-row, air-cooled turbo super charged Wright R-2600-9 Cyclone 14 1,700hp (takeoff) radial engines |
| First flight | 25 February 1941; pilot, Edward W."Ed" Virgin |

## B-25B (Mitchell I) Specifications

| | |
|---|---|
| Model number | NA-62B |
| Number built | 119 (one crashed before delivery; not counted in total—thus, 119) |
| Type | Five-place, medium-class, twin-engine bombardment airplane |
| Wingspan | 67ft, 7in |
| Wing area | 610sq-ft |
| Length | 52ft, 11in |
| Height | 15ft, 9in |
| Empty weight | 20,000lb |
| Maximum weight | 28,460lb |
| Maximum speed | 300mph@15,000ft |
| Maximum range | 1,300mi with 916gal fuel and 3,000lb bomb load (2,900mi ferry range) |
| Service ceiling | 23,500ft |
| Climb rate | 1,704fpm |
| Armament | Two .50cal machine guns in top turret; two .50cal machine guns in bottom turret; one flexible .30cal machine gun in nose |
| Powerplant | Two fourteen-cylinder, twin-row, air-cooled turbo supercharged Wright R-2600-9 Cyclone 14, 1,700hp (take off) radial engines |
| First flight | 1941 (specific date unknown); pilot, unknown |

## XB-28, XB-28A, and B-28 Specifications

| | |
|---|---|
| Model numbers | NA-63, NA-67, and NA-89 |
| Number built | Two XB-28s; one XB-28A; zero B-28s |
| Type | Five-place, twin-engine, medium-class, high-altitude bombardment airplane |
| Wingspan | 72ft, 7in |
| Wing area | 676sq-ft |
| Length | 56ft, 5in |
| Height | 14ft, 0in |
| Empty weight | 25,575lb (XB-28) |
| Maximum weight | 37,200lb (XB-28) |
| Maximum speed | 372mph@25,000ft (XB-28) |
| Maximum range | 2,040mi with 600lb bomb load; maximum bomb load was 4,000lb (XB-28) |
| Service ceiling | 34,600ft (XB-28) |
| Climb rate | 1,111fpm (XB-28) |
| Armament | Three fixed .30cal machine guns in nose; two .50cal machine guns in tail; two .50cal machine guns in top turret; and two .50cal machine guns in bottom turret (XB-28) |
| Powerplant | Two eighteen-cylinder, twin-row, air-cooled turbo super charged Pratt & Whitney R-2800-11 Double Wasp 2,000hp (takeoff) radial engines (XB-28); two Pratt & Whitney R-2800-27s for the XB-28A |
| First flight | 24 April 1942; pilot, Ed Virgin (XB-28) 17 April 1943; pilot, unknown (XB-28A) |

*Author's note:* The XB-28A (NA-67) was a proposed photographic reconnaissance airplane; US-AAC serial numbers ranged from 40-3056 to 40-3058; no B-28s were ordered.

Cable-wound cranks (one on either side of the bomb bay) were used to hoist 2,000lb M34 gravity bombs upward into the B-25; only one could be carried. *Rockwell*

# Chapter 3

# USAAF Mitchell Variants: B-25C to B-25J

While undergoing numerous development programs at NAA from 1939 to 1945, the five- to six-place B-25 Mitchell proved to be an outstanding twin-engine medium-class bomber. And, of course, after the morale-boosting attack on Japan by the B-25Bs of Doolittle's raiders, the USAAF was sold on the B-25 and its constantly expanding list of combat capabilities. It soon became a favorite of the United States' Naval Air Forces and US Allied Air Forces. The high regard for the B-25, B-25A, and B-25B continued through a number of other successful Mitchell variants.

Since NAA's Model NA-40B airplane had served so successfully as the matrix that molded the Model NA-62, the B-25, there was no need to build either "X" (experimental) or "Y" (service test) examples of the original B-25 airplane. In fact, to initiate production, NAA only needed to provide engineering drawings, produce wind-tunnel models, build a full-scale engineering mockup, and build a static structural proof loads test airframe. And NAA's first buyer, the USAAC-cum-USAAF, never regretted

The third production B-25C (NA-82) airplane wings beside the first production Mustang I (NA-83) destined to serve with the RAF. This B-25C, though it has RAF markings on its tail, would later go into battle in the Mediterranean Theater of Operations. *Rockwell*

procuring the B-25 type airplane. Moreover, no other buyer of the Mitchell rejected its performance or combat capabilities.

## The B-25C

NAA's Inglewood facility manufactured 1,625 B-25C airplanes in six developmental blocks—the B-25C-1-NA, B-25C-5-NA, B-25C-10-NA, B-25C-15-NA, B-25C-20-NA, and B-25C-25-NA in production lots of 863 (NA-82), 162 (NA-90), 150 (NA-93), 150 (NA-94), and 300 (NA-96) The B-25C variant of the Mitchell featured powerplant, armament and other improvements over its B-25B counterpart. It was the first mass-produced version of the airplane.

Piloted by NAA's Ed Virgin on 9 November 1941, the premier B-25C (41-12434) was flight tested at Mines Field. With more reliable Wright R-2600-13 Cyclone 14 engines and more effective armament, the B-25C was combat-ready when it reached its user squadrons. The first B-25C airplane was accepted in December 1941, and the last B-25C was accepted in May 1943.

A number of B-25C airplanes were extensively modified for ongoing research and development designed to improve its effectiveness under all operating conditions. From Russia to Rabaul, from England to Egypt—the B-25 Mitchell was used everywhere.

For improved performance in colder climates, for example, two B-25C air-

planes were used for anti-icing and de-icing experiments. These programs created the XB-25E and the XB-25F airplanes (see below). And to evaluate the proposed use of four-bladed propellers, the first B-25C-15-NA (42-32383) was made available.

In any event, during B-25C development and production, many changes came about to improve the type. These, in part, are as follows:

• Incorporation of a Holley carburetor on the R-2600-13 engine, replacing the unreliable Bendix unit.
• Installation of anti-icing and de-icing systems.
• Adoption of a 24-volt electrical system.
• Redesigned bomb racks to incorporate Type 2 electrical releases.
• Stronger outer wing panel structures (heavier extrusion and skin assemblies).
• Change from low- to high-pressure hydraulic wheel brakes.
• Increased fuel capacity by the addition of self-sealing fuel cells in the outboard end of the wing center section.
• Adoption of carburetor air-filtering units.
• Addition of a star-scanning blister above navigator's compartment.
• Installation of Bendix amplidyne machine gun turrets.
• Addition of four (two under either wing) bomb racks.

A fine color study of an early B-25C. But there is something different about this particular airplane. Note upper gun turret location aft of the cockpit. The upper gun turret on B-25C-type airplanes was located much further aft, between the wings and tails. This is one rare bird! *Rockwell*

Fill 'er up! A standard B-25C takes on fuel and air at Inglewood prior to a flight. The C version of the B-25 was the first mass-produced Mitchell. *Rockwell*

• Structural and electrical redesign for installation of a ventral (on centerline) torpedo rack.

• Incorporation of one fixed .50cal machine gun and one flexible .50cal machine gun in bombardier's compartment.

• Installation of fourteen (per engine) flame-dampening engine exhaust pipes (stacks) with related changes.

• Addition of hydraulic emergency landing gear extension (lowering) system.

• Change to a one-piece windshield for improved vision.

• Installation of a 230-gallon self-sealing bomb bay tank.

• Installation of a 325-gallon metal bomb bay tank—every second B-25C airplane only.

## The B-25D (NA-87 and NA-100)

NAA's Kansas City plant manufactured 2,290 B-25D airplanes in eight developmental blocks—the B-25D-1-NC,

An F-10 (formerly a B-25D-30-NC) nicknamed *Pert'nint Poop* at Hickham Field, Hawaii, on 19 March 1946. The F-10s, redesignated RB-25s after the war, were used for mapping and photographic reconnaissance. *David W. Lucabaugh via Ernest R. McDowell*

Excellent color view of a factory-fresh B-25G (NA-96) flying over Southern California. First of the cannon-armed Mitchells, the B-25G was literally a flying arsenal. *Rockwell*

A B-25G fuels up while a Mustang warms up in the background. Classic Standard of California gas tanker truck is noteworthy. *Rockwell*

B-25D-5-NC, B-25D-10-NC, B-25D-15-NC, B-25D-20-NC, B-25D-25-NC, B-25D-30-NC, and B-25D-35-NC in production lots of 1,200 (NA-87) and 1,090 (NA-100). Except for being produced at a different location, the B-25D airplane was identical to the B-25C airplane.

Flown by NAA's Paul Balfour on 3 January 1942, the premier B-25D (41-29648) made its first flight at Fairfax Field. The first B-25D airplane was accepted in February 1942, and the last B-25D airplane was accepted in March 1944.

As listed above, all improvements on the B-25C were also enjoyed by the B-25D. And like the former, the latter

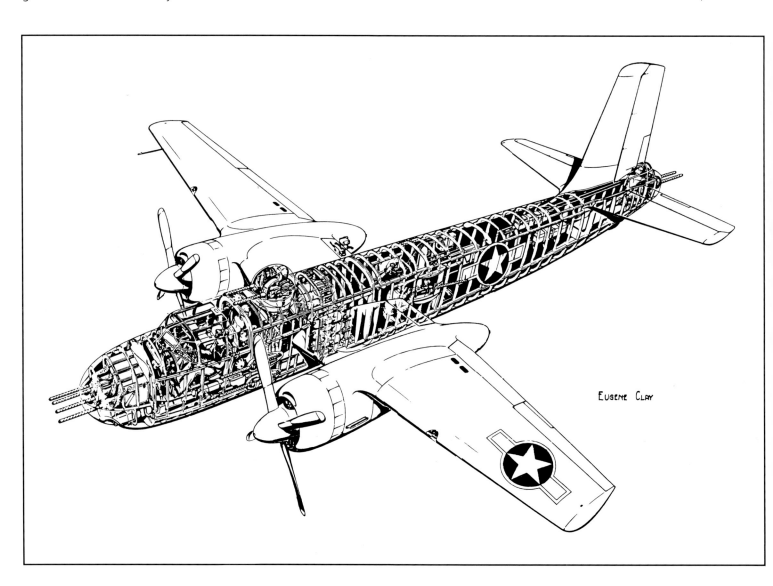

EUGENE CLAY

Once proposed as a single-tail airplane to be powered with two Pratt & Whitney R-2800 engines, the B-25H finally appeared like its predecessors—that is, with twin tails and powered by two Wright R-2600 engines. *Rockwell* was combat ready when received by user squadrons.

## The F-10

In early 1943, because of its ongoing need for high-speed reconnaissance aircraft, the USAAF authorized NAA to convert forty-five Kansas City-built B-25D airplanes into unarmed geographical survey aircraft. In addition to mapping lesser-known terrain—those affected by war—these aircraft were to assess pre- and post-strike enemy positions with an array of onboard photographic equipment. This special version of the B-25D was designated F-10 (the prefix "F" meaning Reconnaissance-Photographic at the time; in the late forties, the prefix "F" was changed to "R," meaning Reconnaissance, and, surviving postwar F-10s were redesignated RB-25D).

To create the F-10 aircraft, following a modest redesign program at NAA's Inglewood facility, NAA's Kansas City workers removed completed B-25D airplanes off the production line. After being towed over to the Modification Center, also located at Fairfax Field, they were modified by, first, the installation of 1,700hp (takeoff) Wright R-2600-29 engines and, second, the incorporation of three synchronized K-17 6in diameter cameras (one in the floor of the nose, and one on either side of the nose); this was called the Trimetrogen Mapping System. During service, a single F-10 airplane cruising at 200mph at an altitude of 10,000ft could map andΔ photograph some 20,000 square miles of territory in a single mission.

## The XB-25E: "Flamin' Maimie"

NAA developed the one-of-a-kind XB-25E (42-32281), otherwise known as the "Flamin' Maimie," to evaluate an improved engine exhaust gas-driven anti-icing system for B-25 aircraft and other medium- to heavy-class bomber and transport aircraft being used in colder climates.

To create this improved anti-icing system, using exhaust gases from its two engines, NAA engineers developed exhaust gas-heated air exchangers capable of producing 10,000BTUs (British thermal units) of heat per hour per pound of heat exchanger weight. In this way, through a series of tubes and slots, all leading and trailing edges of the XB-

The business end of a B-25H with its ten forward-firing .50-caliber machine guns and 75mm cannon looms on the cover of *North American Skyline* magazine. . *Rockwell*

A Wright Aeronautical Company R-2600 Cyclone 14, or Double Cyclone, radial piston engine and a worker pose on a dolly outside the North American Inglewood plant near a brand-new B-25C. From drafting to turning wrenches, women did a lot more than rivet during World War II. *Rockwell*

25E's flying surfaces—wings and tails—were heated enough to ward off the buildup of ice.

During some two years of development and testing through 1944, the XB-25E demonstrated that NAA's anti-icing system worked. But since the end of the war was in sight, no B-25E airplanes were ordered.

Four different versions of the Mitchell line up for a family portrait at NAA's Kansas City plant. From bottom to top are a glass nose B-25J for the USAAF, a glass nose B-25J for the Russian Air Force, a B-25H for the USAAF, and a PBJ-1J for the USN/USMC. The B-25H, not produced at Kansas City, was flown-in from NAA's Inglewood plant. Hangars are part of the Modification Center at NAA's Kansas City plant. *Rockwell*

## The XB-25F

Another one-of-a-kind B-25C airplane, designated XB-25F (unknown serial and block numbers), was modified by NAA to evaluate another type of deicing system whereby electrically-heated elements would eliminate ice build-up on the leading edges of the wings and tails. These elements, tightly wound wires within the leading edges of the airplane's flying surfaces, were fully insulated with asbestos for fireproofing.

## The B-25G (NA-96)

Under the above NA-number, NAA's Inglewood plant produced 400 B-25G airplanes in three development blocks—the B-25G-1-NA, B-25G-5-NA, and B-25-10-NA. The first B-25G airplane was accepted in May 1943 and the last B-25G airplane was accepted in August 1943.

The last production NA-82 B-25C (41-13296) served as the prototype example of the B-25G. Piloted by NAA's Ed Virgin, it made its first flight on 22 October 1942 at Mines Field.

The B-25G featured armament and armor improvements among a number of other design refinements listed below:

• Increased fuel capacity to 434 gallons (normal load), 1,555 gallons (maximum load).

• Additional armament with installation of a single M4 75mm cannon, and two fixed nose-mounted .50cal M3 machine guns.

• Additional armor: 3/8in plate forward of instrument panel; 11/32in deflection plates on lower windshield (3/8in on left of pilot, 3/8in on right of cannoneer); 3/8in plate at pilot's back; 1/4in and 3/8in plating to protect 75mm ammunition box; and armor for top turret gunner.

## The B-25H (NA-98)

Under the above NA-number, NAA's Inglewood plant produced 1,000 B-25H airplanes in three development blocks—the B-25H-1-NA, B-25H-5-NA, and B-25H-10-NA. Essentially, with little or no change as discussed below, these were Kansas City-built B-25Gs. The first B-25H airplane was accepted in August 1943, and the last B-25H airplane was accepted eleven months later in July 1944.

A B-25C-10-NA (42-32372) was modified to serve as the B-25H proto-

type. Nicknamed "Mortimer II," in remembrance of the field-modified strafer prototype dubbed "Mortimer," the prototype B-25H was powered by the Wright R-2600-20 engine. Piloted by NAA's Ed Virgin, the prototype made its first flight on 15 May 1943. The first production B-25H (43-4105), with NAA's Robert C. "Bob" Chilton at the controls, made its first flight on 31 July 1943 at Mines Field. Even though the R-2600-20 engine had powered the B-25H prototype, the R-2600-13 engine powered all production examples of the B-25H. The B-25H version of the Mitchell featured a number of improvements:

• Additional armament: one fixed T13E1 75mm cannon (in place of the B-25G's heavier M4 75mm cannon); two flexible .50cal machine guns in upper turret (moved from aft fuselage section to forward fuselage section); two fixed .50cal blister-type machine guns on either side of the forward fuselage; two flexible .50cal machine guns for firing from either waist gun window in the aft fuselage area; four fixed .50cal machine

An armorer cleans the .50-caliber machine guns in the solid eight-gun nose of a B-25J of the 500th BS, 345th BG at Clark AAF, Luzon, Philippine Islands, on 25 June 1945. *USAF via Ernest R. McDowell*

guns in the nose; and a tail turret with two flexible .50cal machine guns.

• Installation of an aim-pointing gun camera.

• Deletion of copilot's station, which now became the 75mm cannoneer's station.

• Complete rearrangement and front mounting of all pilot's instrumentation.

• Installation of improved electric bomb release controls.

## The Super Strafer

Since it was an unproved engine in early 1939 and would not even be tested in-flight until mid-1940, NAA's propulsion engineers did not recommend the adoption of the air-cooled Pratt & Whitney R-2800 Double Wasp

Sporting near-new A-2 leather jackets, a pilot and copilot illustrate a B-25Cs side-by-side cockpit seating arrangement. *Rockwell via Ernest R. McDowell*

radial engine for the B-25's propulsion system. Pratt & Whitney's proposed two-row, 2,800ci, eighteen-cylinder engine, with turbosupercharging and water injection, was to develop over 2,800hp—more than one horsepower per cubic inch. It featured an improved supercharger and emerged as one of the more powerful engines of the 1940s.

In 1939, however, NAA did not want to gamble on an untried powerplant. In 1943, after NAA realized that the R-2800 had become a hallmark engine, and with the authority given by the USAAF engineering department at Wright Field, it took the 302nd B-25H (43-4406) off the production line to create the Super Strafer, known as model NA-98X. In addition to the other alterations discussed below, its intended Wright R-2600-13 engines were substituted with two Pratt & Whitney 2,000hp R-2800-51 Double Wasp engines. Its bullet-nosed propeller spinners, squared-off wing tips and high-speed air induction cowlings became the primary external changes between the NA-98X and the standard B-25H.

With a projected gross weight of 34,000lb, top speed of the NA-98X was to be 300mph at military power with a sea-level rate of climb of 1,800 feet per minute (fpm); top speed with war emergency power was to be 325mph.

Other notable improvements by NAA to create the one-of-a-kind Super Strafer airplane—in hope of a production order—are as follows:

• Installation of a computing gun sight for the eight fixed nose-mounted .50cal machine guns.

• Installation of a compensating gun sight for the two flexible .50cal tail turret machine guns.

• Addition of illuminated reflector-type optical gun sights for the two .50cal waist machine guns (one on either side of the aft fuselage).

• Incorporation of the NAA-engineered low-drag canopy for the top tur-

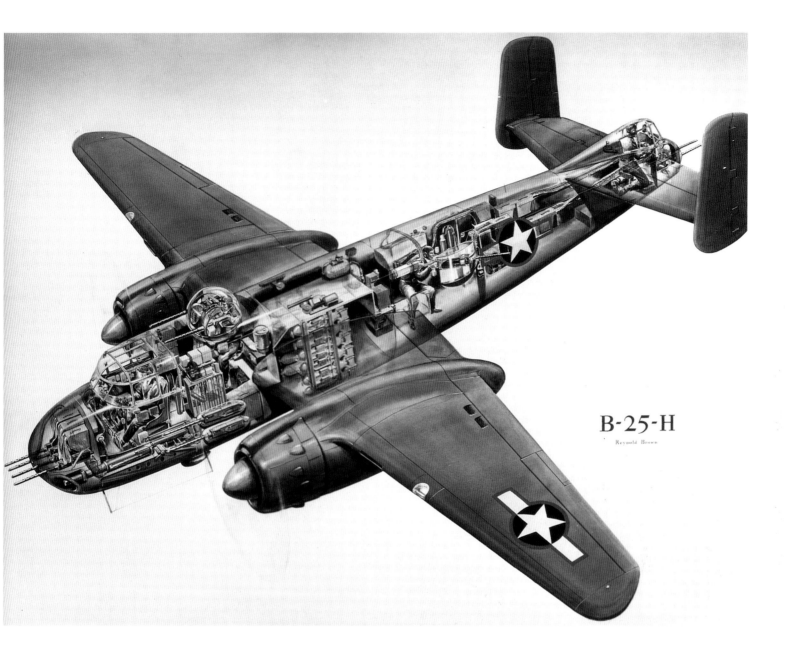

B-25-H

Reynold Brown

ret equipped with two flexible .50cal machine guns.

• Revised flight controls to reduce excessive stick forces.

• A 1.4sq-ft area increase to the ailerons to compensate for the new P-51 Mustang style squared-off wing tips.

• Installation of a 21-gallon tank for an antidetonating fluid to provide up to fifteen minutes of water injection at war emergency power.

Without the standard B-25H blister machine gun packs on either side of the fuselage, the NA-98X was armed with ten .50cal machine guns and one 75mm cannon. The unique 98X was completed in March 1944 and prepared for flight test activities.

On 31 March, with NAA test pilot Joe Barton in the pilot seat, the maiden flight of the Super Strafer prototype was successfully accomplished at Mines Field. Subsequently, Barton bragged of even higher speed and acceleration numbers than had been predicted. In addition, he reported reduced engine vibration and increased roll rate. The airplane was flown to a top speed of 350mph in a dive where no buffeting or instability occurred. Its climb rate was a fantastic 2,040fpm with war emergency power, and 1,886fpm with military power. Using war emergency power, it hit a climb rate of 1,829fpm to reach an altitude of 15,000ft. These performance tests were flown at a 29,000lb gross

Phantom view of the proposed R-2800-powered NA-98X that became the R-2600-powered NA-98 (B-25H). *Rockwell*

weight and, as all those involved agreed, this was one very hot Mitchell.

The NA-98X was also flown by NAA chief test pilot Ed Virgin, USAAF pilots Maj. Otto McIver, Captains McFadden and Fountain, and Royal Air Force squadron leader Hartford. In retrospect, it appeared that the British were also interested in this version of the B-25.

After turning heads with its excellent performance, flight tests of 98X proceeded at Mines Field. Then tragedy struck NAA's Super Strafer program.

"Mortimer" evolved through a series of field modifications to create dedicated strafer-type Mitchells based on the B-25C; the airplane itself being the tenth B-25C (41-12443). *Rockwell*

Wright Field's Flight Test Branch scheduled a series of performance, stability, and control tests and assigned US-AAF officers Maj. Perry Ritchie and F/Lt. Winton Wey to the 98X project. On 24 April 1944, after these men had completed a number of flights on the 98X airplane, Major Ritchie, as he had done previously after all flights, finished this day's flight with a high-speed, low-level pass over NAA's flight ramp followed with a steep spiral pull up. Coming in from the west, Ritchie pulled up as usual. At about 200ft, both of the outer wing structures ripped off the engine nacelles and, immediately afterward, they impacted the tail assembly and tore it off completely. In a matter of seconds, with no time to bail out of the wingless and tailless fuselage, the plane crashed to destruction and both crewmen were killed. Considered to be qualified but somewhat "dramatic," Ritchie, as later concluded, had exceeded 98X's structural limitations.

Although the airplane itself was not at fault, the USAAF opted to not proceed with the 98X airplane and no production contract was forthcoming. Also, even though the Pratt & Whitney R-2800 had boosted performance substantially, no other B-25s were produced with Double Wasp engines. Instead, all versions of the B-25 stayed married to the engines they had been designed to use from the outset —the Wright R-2600 Cyclone 14 which, as it turned out, was not such a bad selection after all.

### The B-25J (NA-108)

Under the above NA-number, NAA's Kansas City plant produced 4,318 B-25J airplanes in eight development blocks— the B-25J-1-NC, B-25J-5-NC, B-25J-10-NC, B-25J-15-NC, B-25J-20-NC, B-25J-25-NC, B-25J-30-NC, and B-25J-35-NC. As the Kansas City-built B-25D was nearly identical to the Inglewood-built B-25C, the Kansas City-built B-25J was nearly identical to the Inglewood-built B-25H.

Piloted by NAA's Joe Barton on 14 December 1943, the first B-25J (43-3870) was flight tested at Fairfax Field. Powered by the R-2600-13 engine, the first B-25J airplane was accepted in December 1943 and the last B-25J airplane was accepted in August 1945. Due to the war's end, an additional seventy-two in-

complete but flyable B-25Js had been built, but they were not accepted contractually. Therefore, Kansas City actually built a total of 4,390 B-25J airplanes. There were two major types of B-25J aircraft: first, a dedicated bomber with a glass nose and, second, a dedicated strafer with a fixed eight-gun solid nose. Additional refinements are as follows:

• Increased armament: four fixed .50cal blister-type machine guns (two on either side of the forward fuselage; one fixed .50cal machine gun and one flexible .50cal machine gun (glass nosed

version); eight fixed .50cal machine guns (solid nosed version); two flexible .50cal machine guns in upper turret; two flexible .50cal waist-type machine guns (one on either side of the aft fuselage section); and two flexible .50cal machine guns in tail turret for a total of twelve guns on the glass nosed version and eighteen guns on the solid nosed version.

• Installation of electrically operated bomb racks and bomb bay doors.

• Incorporation of armor plate protection for bombardier.

Beautiful from any angle, an early production B-25B is profiled from above as it flies southward along California's coastline. Tapered wings, underslung engine nacelles, twin tails, and cigar-shaped fuselage illustrate the B-25's basic airframe structure. Large area elevators are noteworthy. *Rockwell*

• Incorporation of improved armor-plated pilot's and copilot's seats.
• Altered pilot's instrumentation.
• Capability to carry three 1,000lb bombs instead of two as before.

Four-gun strafer nose mockup of proposed version of the B-25C-10-NA (NA-94). This proposed arrangement, though not adopted on factory-built B-25C/Ds, came to life on the B-25H-type Mitchell. *Rockwell*

• Capability of carrying two armor-piercing 1,600lb bombs.

## The Strafer-Bomber

On 17 March 1944, NAA's Inglewood engineering department completed a presentation pamphlet on a new type of Strafer-Bomber airplane based on the B-25J (NA-108) version of the Mitchell. With the approval of NAA management, the Strafer-Bomber idea

A B-25C-25-NA with the final finger-type engine exhaust stacks (pipes). On nighttime missions, flame from early B-25 engine exhaust stacks were easily spotted by enemy gunners. This arrangement was the answer. *Rockwell*

Very rare view of a B-25 with four-bladed propellers (ala B-26) that were not adopted. *Rockwell*

was presented to the USAAF. In part, NAA's unsolicited presentation stated:

The following data reveal the possibility of providing a fast and versatile medium bomber fitted with two Pratt & Whitney R-2800-51 engines that may be used for a variety of missions. Although this airplane may be arranged in any of several versions, it will retain the best features of the Model B-25 Series Airplane and in addition will provide added power, improved performance, and greater offensive and defensive armament.

Four droppable Aerojet rocket-assisted take-off bottles—mounted to this B-25's underwing bomb shackles—rapidly boost this Mitchell's take-off at Wright AAF. These tests were conducted by the Air Technical Service Command (ATSC) at Wright Field. Though acceptable, this mode of take-off for B-25s was not known to be used operationally. *USAF*

Fine color study of a manned tail gun position on a B-25 or B-25A. *USAF*

Equipped with a strafing nose and demolition or fragmentation bomb racks, it is, because of its speed and maneuverability, a formidable airplane for use against ground installation and troops. Furnished with a bombardier's nose and bombing equipment it is well suited for fast precision bombing.

As proposed, the Strafer-Bomber was to have a five-man crew: pilot, navigator, flight engineer/gunner, radio operator/waist gunner, and tail gunner.

Its maximum armament, as projected, was to be eighteen .50cal machine guns with 7,200 total rounds of ammunition. This consisted of eight fixed for- ward-firing nose guns (400 rounds each), four fixed forward-firing side guns (400 rounds each), two flexible upper turret guns (400 rounds each), two flexible waist guns (200 rounds each), and two flexible tail turret guns (600 rounds each). The twelve forward-firing nose guns would use the K-14 gun sight, the two upper turret guns would use the K-9 gun sight, the two waist guns would use the N-8A gun sight, and the two tail turret guns would use the K-10 gun sight. The upper turret would be the Type A-9A Bendix unit with an improved low-drag turret canopy with a streamlined transparent fairing, and the tail turret would be the Type M-7 Bell unit; waist guns were to be of the Gerrity type.

The bomb bay racks could carry the following: two 1,600lb armor-piercing bombs; or, four 1,000lb bombs; or, six 800lb or 900lb armor-piercing bombs; or, three 650lb depth charges; or, six 600lb armor-piercing bombs; or, eight 500lb semi-armor-piercing bombs; or, six 500lb bombs; or, six 325lb depth charges; or, eight 250lb bombs; or, eight 300lb bombs; or, twelve 100lb bombs.

North American's proposed Strafer-Bomber, though it was neither built nor flown, could have been and probably would have been—that is, without hanging turbojet engines on it—the *ultimate* B-25.

## Armament and Radar Systems

As dedicated bombardment and patrol aircraft, the B-25 and PBJ airplanes

were optimized throughout their careers to fly and fight with a wide variety of armament and radar systems. These included the following:

• The M2 .30cal machine gun; fixed or movable in varied numbers up to three.

• The M2 .50cal machine gun; fixed or movable in varied numbers up to fourteen.

• The M3 .50cal machine gun; fixed or movable in varied numbers up to eighteen.

• One M4 75mm cannon; fixed (twenty-one rounds).

• One T13E1 75mm cannon; fixed (twenty-one rounds).

• Two 11.75in diameter Tiny Tim rocket.

• Eight 5in diameter fixed-fin rockets (four under either wing).

• Six 300lb depth charges (three under either wing).

• Twelve M8 4.5in diameter folding-fin rockets; three under either wing in launching tubes, three on either side of the fuselage in launching tubes.

• One 4,150lb Mk13 glide torpedo.
• One 2,000lb GB-1 glide bomb.
• One GB-13 glide bomb.
•Various combinations and amounts of AP (all purpose) and GP (general purpose) free-falling 100lb, 250lb, 300lb, 500lb, 600lb, 1,000lb, 1,100lb, 1,600lb, and 2,000lb gravity bombs.

Other known armaments included incendiary bombs and antishipping mines. In addition, the B-25 and the PBJ employed several different types of radar systems. These included the following:

• The AN/APQ-7 Eagle Radar Wing system for navigation and high-altitude bombardment; this radar was coupled to the Norden bombsight via a "Nosmeagle."

• The AN/APQ-13 Radar radome system for navigation and high-altitude bombardment.

• The Bombardment Through Overcast (BTO) Radar system for navigation and the detection and destruction of land-based enemy targets in bad weather from various altitudes.

Ordnance specialists prepare to load a bomb bay with 100lb bombs for yet another mission. *USAF*

The AN/APQ-7, AN/APQ-13 and BTO radar systems were employed by USAAF B-25s; the AN/APS-3 radar system was used on USMC PBJs. The -7 and -13 systems were carried ventrally amidships on B-25s while the BTO unit was mounted under the nose of the B-25, protruding ahead of it. The -3 system was either carried on the upper nose or on the right wing tip of PBJ aircraft.

## Summary

With the above mentioned changes, in addition to continued refinements, the B-25 remained a top-ranking medium-class bombardment and strafing aircraft throughout World War II. Moreover, as can be seen, it had been fitted for perhaps more different types of tactical operations than any other plane in its class for the time period. The most spectacular of the changes being the

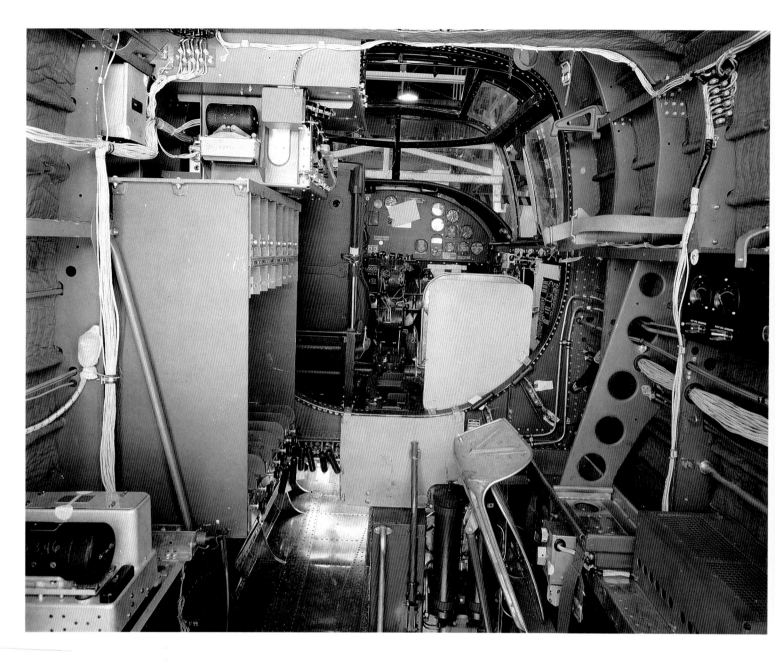

B-25H cockpit shows nose gun and cannon operator's position to the right of the pilot's seat; there was no copilot. *Rockwell*

successful incorporation of a 75mm (2.95in) cannon in the nose sections of the B-25G and B-25H model airplanes. These were the first aircraft in the world to successfully carry and use such a large weapon. Although the tactical significance of this installation was later reduced by the development of high-explosive warhead rockets (guided and unguided), the 75mm cannon-equipped B-25s proved to be extremely effective during certain attack operations, and es-

pecially against shipping in the Southwest Pacific.

Even without including the 75mm cannon installation on the B-25G/H models, several other versions of the B-25 constituted some of the most heavily armed aircraft in the world. The last version of the Mitchell—the solid nosed B-25J—was capable of carrying eighteen .50cal machine guns with 7,200 rounds of .50cal ammunition. This *attack* type of the B-25 was more heavily armed than the Boeing B-29 Superfortress or other large four-engine heavy-class bombardment airplanes. The bottom line: As a war machine, the B-25 was first rate.

All in all at two manufacturing facilities—Inglewood and Kansas City—NAA produced 9,889 B-25 Mitchell airplanes in eight major versions—the B-25, B-25A, B-25B, B-25C, B-25D, B-25G, B-25H, and the B-25J. From these major build models came the series of derivative types—the Mitchell I, II, and III series; the Advanced Trainer or AT-24A/B/C/D series; and the PBJ-1/-1C/-1D/-1G/-1H/-1J series. In addition there were some experimental B-25s produced to investigate evolving anti-icing, de-icing, propulsion, and weapon and radar systems. For the most part, though, nearly 10,000 Mitchells were built (the highest number of any World

War II medium-class bomber plane), the basic airframe structure and propulsion system of the B-25 changed little during the entire course of its five-year manufacturing program—from early 1940 to late 1945.

## B-25C (Mitchell II) Specifications

| | |
|---|---|
| Model numbers | NA-82, NA-90, NA-93, NA-94, and NA-96 |
| Number built | 1,625 |
| Type | Five-place, medium-class, twin-engine bombardment airplane |
| Wingspan | 67ft, 7in |
| Wing area | 610sq-ft |
| Length | 52ft, 11in |
| Height | 15ft, 10in |
| Empty weight | 20,300lb |
| Maximum weight | 34,000lb |
| Maximum speed | 284mph @ 15,000ft |
| Maximum range | 1,500mi with 916gal fuel and 3,000lb bomb load |
| Service ceiling | 21,200ft |
| Climb rate | 909fpm |
| Armament | Two .50cal machine guns in top turret; two .50cal machine guns in bottom turret; one flexible .50cal machine gun in nose; one fixed .50cal machine gun in nose |
| Powerplant | Two fourteen-cylinder, twin-row, air-cooled turbosupercharged Wright R-2600-13 Cyclone 14 1,700hp (takeoff) radial engines |
| First flight | 9 November 1941; pilot, Ed Virgin |

## B-25D (Mitchell II) Specifications

| | |
|---|---|
| Model numbers | NA-87 and NA-100 |
| Number built | 2,290 |
| Type | Five-place, medium-class, twin-engine bombardment airplane |
| Wingspan | 67ft, 7in |
| Wing area | 610sq-ft |
| Length | 52ft, 11in |
| Height | 15ft, 10in |
| Empty weight | 20,300lb |
| Maximum weight | 34,000lb |
| Maximum speed | 284mph @ 15,000ft |
| Maximum range | 1,500mi with 916gal fuel and 3,000lb bomb load |
| Service ceiling | 21,200ft |
| Climb rate | 909fpm |

Field nose gun maintenance on a solid-nose B-25J at Tacloban, circa February 1945. *Vic Tatelman Collection via Jeff Ethell*

An upper twin-fifty machine gun turret, which it appears here, is being explained to a worker that will install them. Note the .50cal machine gun rounds. *Rockwell*

| | |
|---|---|
| Wing area | 613.9sq-ft |
| Length | 53ft, 5-3/4in |
| Height | 16ft, 4-3/16in |
| Empty weight | 19,800lb |
| Maximum weight | 32,275lb |
| Maximum speed | 300mph @ 20,000ft |
| Maximum range | 3,000mi |
| Service ceiling | 25,000ft |
| Climb rate | 2,000fpm |
| Armament | None |
| Powerplant | Two fourteen-cylinder, twin-row, air-cooled turbosupercharged Wright R-2600-29 Cyclone 14 1,700hp (takeoff) radial engines |
| First flight | Unknown; pilot, unknown |

## B-25G Specifications

| | |
|---|---|
| Model number | NA-96 |
| Number built | 400 |
| Type | Five-place, medium-class, twin-engine attack and bombardment airplane |
| Wingspan | 67ft, 7in |
| Wing area | 610sq-ft |
| Length | 51ft, 0in |
| Height | 15ft, 9in |
| Empty weight | 19,975lb |
| Maximum weight | 35,000lb |
| Maximum speed | 281mph @ 15,000ft |
| Maximum range | 2,450mi (ferry) |
| Service ceiling | 24,300ft |
| Climb rate | 967fpm |
| Armament | One fixed 75mm cannon in nose; two fixed .50cal machine guns in nose; two .50cal blister machine guns on right side of fuselage; two flexible .50cal machine guns in upper turret; two .50cal waist machine guns; two .50cal tail turret machine guns |
| Powerplant | Two fourteen-cylinder, twin-row, air-cooled turbosupercharged Wright R-2600-13 Cyclone 14 1,700hp (takeoff) radial engines |
| First flight | 22 October 1942; pilot, Ed Virgin |

| | |
|---|---|
| Armament | Two .50cal machine guns in top turret; two .50cal machine guns in bottom turret; one flexible .50cal machine gun in nose; one fixed .50cal machine gun in nose |
| Powerplant | Two fourteen-cylinder, twin-row, air-cooled turbosupercharged Wright R-2600-13 Cyclone 14 1,700hp (takeoff) radial engines |
| First flight | 3 January 1942; pilot, Paul Balfour |

## F-10 Specifications

| | |
|---|---|
| Model numbers | NA-87 and NA-100 |
| Number built | 45 (ten new builds; thirty-five modified B-25D airplanes) |
| Type | Five-place, medium-class, twin-engine photographic reconnaissance airplane |
| Wingspan | 67ft, 6.7in |

## B-25H Specifications

| | |
|---|---|
| Model number | NA-98 |
| Number built | 1,000 |
| Type | Five-place, medium-class, twin-engine attack and bombardment airplane |
| Wingspan | 67ft, 7in |
| Wing area | 610sq-ft |
| Length | 51ft, 0in |
| Height | 15ft, 9in |

FIG. 27

## WING BOMB RACKS

| | |
|---|---|
| Empty weight | 19,975lb |
| Maximum weight | 33,500lb |
| Maximum speed | 275mph @ 13,000ft |
| Maximum range | 2,700mi (ferry) |
| Service ceiling | 24,800ft |
| Climb rate | 789fpm |
| Armament | One fixed 75mm cannon in nose; four fixed .50cal machine guns in nose; four .50cal blister machine guns on either side of fuselage; two flexible .50cal machine guns in upper turret; two .50cal waist machine guns; two .50cal tail turret machine guns |
| Powerplant | Two fourteen-cylinder, twin-row, air-cooled turbosupercharged Wright R-2600-13 Cyclone 14 1,700hp (takeoff) radial engines |

| | |
|---|---|
| First flight | 15 May 1943; pilot, Ed Virgin |

### Super Strafer Prototype Specifications

| | |
|---|---|
| Model number | NA-98X |
| Number built | 1; crashed to destruction 24 April 1944 |
| Type | Five-place, medium-class, twin-engine bombardment and strafer airplane |
| Wingspan | 67ft, 7in |
| Wing area | 610sq-ft |
| Length | 51ft, 0in |
| Height | 15ft, 9in |
| Empty weight | 21,475lb |
| Maximum weight | 34,000lb |
| Maximum speed | 346.5mph @ 12,600ft (war emergency power) |
| Maximum range | Projected to be 2,000mi with 974gal fuel and 3,000lb bomb load |
| Service ceiling | Projected to be 25,000ft |

Underwing bomb racks for eight bombs (four under each wing) as depicted for a B-25 Technical Order manual. *USAF*

| | |
|---|---|
| Climb rate | 2,040fpm (war emergency power) |
| Armament | Two .50cal machine guns in top turret; two .50cal machine guns in waist turrets; four .50cal machine guns in nose; two .50cal machine guns in tail turret; one 75mm cannon in nose |
| Powerplant | Two eighteen-cylinder, twin-row, air-cooled turbosupercharged Pratt & Whitney R-2800-41 Double Wasp 2,000hp (takeoff) radial engines |
| First flight | 31 March 1944; pilot, Joe Barton |

## B-25J (Mitchell III) Specifications

| | |
|---|---|
| Model number | NA-108 |
| Number built | 4,318 |
| Type | Six-place, medium-class, twin-engine attack and bombardment airplane |
| Wingspan | 67ft, 6.7in |
| Wing area | 577.67sq-ft |
| Length | 53ft, 5.75in |
| Height | 16ft, 4.19in |
| Empty weight | 19,490lb |
| Maximum weight | 33,400lb |
| Maximum speed | 293mph @ 13,850ft |
| Maximum range | 3,240mi (ferry) |
| Service ceiling | 24,500ft |
| Climb rate | 1,587fpm |
| Armament | Glass nose—one fixed .50cal machine gun, one flexible .50cal machine gun in nose; solid nose—eight fixed .50cal machine guns; two flexible .50cal machine guns in upper turret; two flexible .50cal waist machine guns; two flexible .50cal tail turret machine guns; four fixed .50cal blister machine guns |
| Powerplant | Two fourteen-cylinder, twin-row, air-cooled turbosupercharged Wright R-2600-29 Cyclone 14 |
| | 1,700hp (takeoff) radial engines |
| First flight | 14 December 1943; pilot, Joe Barton |

## Strafer-Bomber Proposal Specifications

| | |
|---|---|
| Model number | NA-108X (tentative) |
| Number built | None |
| Type | Five-place, medium-class, twin-engine strafer and bombardment airplane |
| Wingspan | 67ft, 6.7in |
| Wing area | 613.9sq-ft |
| Length | 53ft, 5-3/4in |
| Height | 16ft, 4-3/16in |

This Kansas City-built B-25D-10-NC (41-30244) has the navigators bubble and top turret like normal; however, the tail cone, waist gun windows, and side pack guns are a mystery. The crudeness of these modifications and the date when these photos were taken (17 January 1944) suggest strongly that these modifications were done in a combat zone; possibly one of the first field modifications *Rockwell*

60

| | |
|---|---|
| Empty weight | 20,500lb |
| Maximum weight | 34,822lb |
| Maximum speed | 325mph @ 20,000ft (projected) |
| Maximum range | 3,225mi (projected) |
| Service ceiling | 25,000ft (projected) |
| Climb rate | 2,500fpm (projected) |
| Armament | Eight .50cal machine guns in nose; four .50cal machine guns in side packs; two .50cal machine guns in top turret; two .50cal waist guns on either side of the fuselage; and two .50cal machine guns in tail turret (maximum) |
| Powerplant | Two eighteen-cylinder, twin-row, air-cooled turbosupercharged Pratt & Whitney R-2800-51 Double Wasp 2,000hp (takeoff) radial engines |

A B-25D, nicknamed *My Buddy*, clearly shows what the ETO Bombing Through Overcast (BTO) radar system antenna looked like. *F. C. Dickey Collection via Ernest R. McDowell*

The glass panel just above the man's head was
the escape hatch on B-25H/J-type airplanes.
*Rockwell*

Artist concept of B-25J strafer at wave-top
height firing side pack, top turret, and nose
guns. *Arden Morris; Rockwell*

A PBJ-1H equipped with two 11.75in diameter "Tiny Tim" aircraft rockets (one on either side of the fuselage) circa April 1945. *Rockwell*

Waist and tail gun installations on a B-25J. *Rockwell*

A B-25H with six M8 4.5in diameter rocket tube bundles of three (three bundles on either side of the fuselage). Similar three-tube bundles could be carried under the wing as well. *Rockwell*

For extended range, either fixed or droppable bomb bay fuel tanks were incorporated in various models of the Mitchell. Shown in this sequence of photographs is a droppable tank being installed and connected. *Rockwell*

Solid eight-gun nose on a B-25J. *Campbell Archives*

A B-25J equipped with the Eagle Radar Wing system. *Rockwell*

NAA workers practice attaching bombs to a B-25H's inboard shackles with an A-frame type hoist. *Rockwell*

Top-to-bottom series of photos shows a PBJ-1H, equipped with the AN/APS-3 search radar (right wing tip) firing an 11.75in "Tiny Tim" rocket. *Rockwell*

*Chapter 4*

# Mitchells in Combat

With his 20/20 vision focused toward the future, Billy Mitchell forewarned the 1920s military establishment—the US Army Air Service in particular—that the airplane would be the primary weapon in the forthcoming decades. Carrying his namesake, the B-25, first appearing some four years after his untimely death, turned out to be everything Mitchell represented. And it was *just* a medium-class bombardment airplane! Extensively modified throughout the course of World War II to meet its ever-changing mission requirements, the B-25 helped vindicate Mitchell who died "a prophet without honor" at the age of fifty-seven on 19 February 1936.

## Allied Forces versus Axis Powers

World War II was many things to many people. But first and foremost, it was an all-out battle between the Allied Forces (the United States, Australia, Belgium, Brazil, Canada, China, Denmark, France, Great Britain, Greece, New Zealand, Norway, Poland, Russia, South Africa, the Netherlands, and Yugoslavia) and the Axis Powers (Bulgaria, Germany, Hungary, Italy, Japan, and Roma-

nia). In the final outcome the Allies prevailed and, wherever it operated, the B-25 proved to be a major asset. In part, the B-25's battle lines were drawn in the theaters and areas as follows:

• American Theater—the contiguous United States, Alaska, Hawaii, and United States Territories such as Puerto Rico.

• Caribbean area—the Bahamas, the West Indies, and so on.

• China-Burma-India (CBI) Theater.

• European-African-Middle Eastern (EAME) Theater—Southern Europe, North Africa, Saudi Arabia, Turkey, Iraq, Iran, Syria, Oman, and so on.

• European Theater of Operations (ETO)—United Kingdom, Ireland, France, Spain, Germany, and so on.

• Mediterranean Theater of Operations (MTO)—Tunisia, Libya, Egypt, Crete, Greece, Italy, and so on.

The B-25D airplane (43-3374) that NAA restored for the tenth anniversary of the Doolittle raid; it is dressed to duplicate Doolittle's B-25B 40-2344). It is now on permanent display at the US Air Force Museum in Dayton, Ohio. *Rockwell*

The USAAC-cum-USAAF ordered 120 B-25B airplanes. One of these, however, crashed before it was delivered to and accepted by its purchaser; thus 119 production B-25Bs. *F. C. Dickey Collection via Ernest R. McDowell*

One of the first "gull-wing" B-25 airplanes (40-2180) of the 17th BG, 34th BS—the "Thunderbirds," squadron number 43—flies near McChord Field, Tacoma, Washington, circa 1941. *USAF via Jeff Ethell*

• North Atlantic area—Greenland, Iceland, and so on.
• Pacific Theater—Northern Marianas, Marshall Islands, Caroline Islands, and so on.
• Southwest Pacific—New Guinea, New Britain, and so on.
• Western Pacific—the Philippines, Borneo, and so on.

There were, of course, more obscure places that Mitchell bombers did battle. They fought everywhere—period.

## Beginnings: Coastal Defense and the Doolittle Raid

Immediately after the attack on Pearl Harbor, Hawaii, on 7 December 1941 different types of land-based aircraft began flying coastal defense missions. Flying out of air bases that were close to the Pacific and Atlantic oceans, these aircraft looked for and destroyed any enemy shipping they could find. The B-25 was one of those aircraft. Even though the Mitchell had not been optimized as a patrol-type bomber plane, especially the very early versions available at the time, they proved well suited to this task. Less than four months after Pearl Harbor, however, Mitchells began to demonstrate their offensive capability. But from a very unlikely place—the pitching and rolling deck of a US Navy aircraft carrier, the USS *Hornet.*

On 18 April 1942, as the *Hornet* sailed eastward toward the island nation of Japan, USAAF ordnance personnel stuffed as many bombs as they could into the bellies of sixteen B-25Bs. The idea was to strike back at Japan for the attack on Pearl Harbor. If successful,

though little more than a slap on its wrist, the strike would let Japan know that its domain was not such a safe haven after all.

The optimum launch point, under the cover of darkness, was to be some 500 miles from Tokyo. The plan was to fly at night, bomb in the early morning, and recover in China the next day. But the *Hornet* was spotted by Japanese picket boats about 670 miles from Japan. One or more of the picket boats communicated the position of the *Hornet* before being sunk.

Adm. William F. "Bull" Halsey, Jr., in charge of the daring operation aboard the USS *Enterprise,* decided to launch the aircraft about 150 miles early after Task Force 16 was sighted by the picket boats. Capt. Marc A. Mitscher, commander of the *Hornet,* gave the order to launch: "Now hear this. The army personnel are going to bomb Japan!" What the sailors did not know was that the Army per-

Lt. Col. James H. "Jimmy" Doolittle, shown lower right, and other USAAF and NAA personnel evaluate bombers for the upcoming secret raid on Japan. The pretty little job at the upper left-hand corner was the winner. *Rockwell*

sonnel would actually strike four Japanese cities before the mission was over—Tokyo, Yokohama, Kobe, and Osaka.

The leader of the sixteen-plane attack, then-Lt. Col. James H. "Jimmy" Doolittle, would go first. And with only

On board the USS *Hornet* (CV 8) as it sails westward across the Pacific Ocean into Japanese waters, Lieutenant Colonel Doolittle (on the left) and carrier commander Capt. Marc A. Mitscher exchange jokes to boost the morale of seventy-nine crewmen before the Doolittle raid. Doolittle's B-25B is shown in the background, and the 500lb bomb was the first of four to be loaded into his plane. *USAF via Rockwell*

With only 467ft of carrier deck runway ahead of him, Doolittle launched from the *Hornet* at 8:15 a.m. local time to begin the 18 April 1942 raid on Japan; the Doolittle Raiders' sixteen B-25Bs hit four Japanese cities. *USAF via Rockwell*

Wooden broom handles were installed as shown to simulate twin .50-caliber machine guns in the tails of the Doolittle B-25Bs that struck Japan in April 1942. *Ernest R. McDowell*

467 ft between his B-25's nose wheel and the bow of the carrier, the crack pilot roared off the pitching deck of the *Hornet*. He circled the carrier once, and after about an hour, the rest of the Billy Mitchells were also airborne and on their way to Japan. They launched in the following order:

1. B-25B (40-2344) manned by Lt. Col. James H. Doolittle, Lt. Richard E. Cole, Lt. Henry A. Potter, S/Sgt. Fred A. Braemer, and S/Sgt. Paul J. Leonard.

2. B-25B (40-2292) manned by Lt. Travis Hoover, Lt. William N. Fitzhugh, Lt. Carl R. Wildner, Lt. Richard E. Miller, and Sgt. Douglas V. Radney.

3. B-25B (40-2270) manned by Lt. Robert M. Gray, Lt. Jacob E. Manch, Lt. Charles J. Ozuk, Sgt. Aden E. Jones, and Cpl. Leland D. Factor.

4. B-25B (40-2282) manned by Lt. Everett W. Holstrom, Lt. Lucien N. Youngblood, Lt. Harry C. McCool, Sgt. Robert J. Stevens, and Cpl. Bert M. Jordan.

5. B-25B (40-2283) manned by Capt. David M. Jones, Lt. Rodney R. Wilder, Lt. Eugene F. McGurl, Lt. Denber V. Truelove, and Sgt. Joseph W. Manske.

6. B-25B (40-2298) manned by Lt. Dean E. Hallmark, Lt. Robert J. Meder, Lt. Chase J. Nielsen, Sgt. William J. Dieter, and Sgt. Donald E. Fitzmaurice.

7. B-25B (40-2261) manned by Lt. Ted W. Lawson, Lt. Dean Davenport, Lt. Charles L. McClure, Lt. Robert S. Clever, and Sgt. David J. Thatcher.

8. B-25B (40-2242) manned by Capt. Edward J. York, Lt. Robert G. Emmens, Lt. Nolan A. Herndon, S/Sgt. T. H. Laban, and Sgt. David W. Pohl.

9. B-25B (40-2303) manned by Lt. Harold F. Watson, Lt. James M. Parker, Lt. Tom C. Griffin, Sgt. Wayne M. Bissel, and T/Sgt. Eldred V. Scott.

10. B-25B (40-2250) manned by Lt. Richard O. Joyce, Lt. J. Royden Stork, Lt. Horace E. Crouch, Sgt. George E. Larkin, Jr., and S/Sgt. Edwin W. Horton.

11. B-25B (40-2249) manned by Capt. C. Ross Greening, Lt. Ken E. Reddy, Lt. Frank J. Kappeler, S/Sgt. William L. Birch, and Sgt. Melvin J. Gardner.

12. B-25B (40-2278) manned by Lt. William M. Bower, Lt. Thadd H. Blanton, Lt. William R. Pound, T/Sgt. Waldo J. Bither, and S/Sgt. Omer H. Duquette.

13. B-25B (40-2247) manned by Lt. Edgar E. McElroy, Lt. Richard A. Knobloch, Lt. Clayton J. Campbell, Sgt.

In the 1944 MGM film *Thirty Seconds Over Tokyo*, a B-25B nicknamed *Ruptured Duck* was featured. Van Johnson played Lawson and Spencer Tracy played Doolittle. *MGM via Campbell Archives*

Robert C. Bourgeois, and Sgt. Adam R. Williams.

14. B-25B (40-2297) manned by Maj. John A. Hilger, Lt. Jack A. Sims, Lt. James H. Macia, S/Sgt. Jacob Eierman, and S/Sgt. Edwin V. Bain.

15. B-25B (40-2267) manned by Lt. Donald G. Smith, Lt. Griffith T. Williams, Lt. Howard A. Sessler, Sgt. Edward

The real *Ruptured Duck* was indeed one of the sixteen B-25Bs (40-2261) used in the Tokyo Raid. Piloted by Lt. Ted W. Lawson (who also wrote the film script), it was the seventh plane to launch that morning. *Rockwell*

An April 1979 illustration by Bob Casey commemorating the Doolittle Raiders. *Rockwell*

J. Saylor, and Lt. Thomas R. White (M.D.).

16. B-25B (40-2268) manned by Lt. William G. Farrow, Lt. Robert L. Hite, Lt. George Barr, Cpl. Jacob deShazer, and Sgt. Harold A. Spatz.

The respective crewmen are listed above in order by pilot, copilot, navigator, bombardier, engineer/gunner, and gunner. Lieutenants Herndon, Macia, and Sessler pulled double duties as bombardiers and navigators.

The sixteen B-25Bs came from the 17th Bombardment Group (Medium), which was made up of the 34th, 37th, 95th, and 89th squadrons. The 89th was a reconnaissance squadron attached to the 17th BG.

Since the aircraft launched much sooner than planned, fuel became a scarce commodity after the raid. Worse, night arrived and there were no lighted runways to recover on. Literally running on empty, and plowing through dark into who knew what, all sixteen aircraft descended.

Fifteen of them crash landed in China or the South China Sea. One landed "safely" in Russia and its five-man crew was interned (Russia was not at war with Japan at the time and, as a result, those crewmen were confined). Out of the other seventy-five crewmen, three died and eight were captured. Most of the crewmen escaped, many after horrid experiences, and returned to the United States. Others were reassigned to fly and fight again.

The essence of patriotism and the epitome of bravery, these eighty men honed the sword of many air battles and tactical surprises to come from the Allied Forces during the course of World War II. The raid was successful and, if nothing else, it greatly boosted dwindling morale in the United States. As rewards for their respective efforts, Doolittle was promoted two ranks to Brigadier General and received the nation's highest award—the Congressional Medal of Honor; his seventy-nine raiders received the Distinguished Flying Cross—the Air Force's eighth-highest medal in order of precedence. More important, these men will never be forgotten for what they did.

In turn the B-25, having been "baptized under fire" in the truest sense of that phrase, had not only finished at the head of the medium-bombardment airplane class, it had demonstrated its unique ability to alter its primary mission to a secondary capability—that of a carrier-based attack plane. As it came about, the raid on four Japanese cities was just a taste of what the B-25 was capable of. And during its four-plus years of combat activities, the Mitchell proved time and time again that it was adaptable to many other uses.

Nearly overnight, what had once been nothing more than a "paper airplane," became the B-25, a warplane in the first degree. Day in and day out, thousands of Mitchell bombers decimated their adversaries at sea, on land, and in the air.

## B-25s In Action

The 17th Bombardment Group (Medium), in the winter of 1941, was the first outfit to receive a B-25. Having just moved to McChord Field, Washington, from March Field, California, the 17th BG (M) at the time was made up of the 34th, 73rd, and 95th squadrons; the 73rd was soon replaced by the 37th. Its first B-25, the fourth unbroken dihedral-wing airplane (40-2168) arrived at McChord Field in February 1941. In March the fifth production B-25, also having the "straight" wing, arrived and was assigned to the 34th Bombardment Squadron—the famed "Thunderbirds." By the end of May the 34th had received four more B-25s, and three of them (40-2180, 40-2186, and 40-2188), featured the new broken dihedral or "gull wing" configuration for improved bombardment accuracy. And by the end of September 1941, the 17th BG had fifty-two B-25, B-25A, and B-25B Mitchell bombers. By this time the 17th had transferred to Pendleton, Oregon.

Interestingly at the time, the USAAF had ten medium-class bombardment groups. And, except for the B-25-equipped 17th and another equipped with Martin B-26s, these groups were outfitted with obsolete Douglas B-18s and B-23s. Following the attack on Pearl Harbor, these groups, including the 17th, were assigned to coastal defense flying

A number of 12th BG B-25C/Ds arrive at Esler Field, Louisiana, from McChord Field, Washington, in March 1942. After months of intensive training, the 12th BG was classified as combat ready and departed for Egypt to do battle in the MTO. *Alex Adair*

Four B-25H/J airplanes of the 12th BG bank right to make their respective bombing runs on axis targets in Southern Italy, circa July 1944. *Alex Adair*

More targets in Southern Italy are bombed by B-25H/Js of the 12th BG, circa July 1944. *Alex Adair*

antisubmarine patrols offshore. They did this until the US Navy and US Marine Corps were equipped with better patrol bombers, including the B-25-derived PBJ airplanes, discussed in chapter seven.

The first Mitchells to see overseas deployment and combat were forty-eight Inglewood-built B-25Cs that had been ferried across the Pacific Ocean to Australia beginning in March 1942. Most of these, originally slated for action in the Dutch East Indies, were assigned to the 3rd BG's 13th and 90th BSs, which arrived in the Philippine Islands in April 1942. A Dutch Air Force squadron (No. 18) and the 13th and 90th squadrons raided Japanese shipping. The 3rd BG, joined by the 38th BG in September 1942, set up operations in the Southwest Pacific flying out of the New Guinea area. Both were assigned to the Fifth Air Force. In June 1943, likewise assigned to the Fifth AF, the 345th BG arrived in the Southwest Pacific area of operations. And shortly thereafter, because the airplane—the Martin B-26 Marauder—needed longer runways and did not have as much range, the 22nd BG converted to B-25s and its B-26s departed for European bases. Thus the 22nd had joined with the 3rd, 38th, and 345th bombardment groups for action in the South Pacific.

Next comes the Tenth Air Force assigned to the CBI Theater of Operations. To begin, two squadrons—the 11th and 22nd—were first to deploy to the CBI area of operations. The 11th BS, first for the 7th BG, arrived in China in June 1942. The 22nd BS, having arrived simultaneously in India, became the first squadron of the 341st BG, which formed three months later. The next bombardment group, the 12th BG, arrived in North Africa (Egypt) in August 1942 as the first B-25-equipped unit to see action in the MTO. Made up of the 81st, 82nd, 83rd and 434th bombard-

Top gun—five, bottom gun—two! Mitchell gunners also earned their spurs in combat and accounted for the demise of many Axis aircraft. Note that the top gun gunner has downed five Japanese aircraft, and as customary with that many kills, he became an ace. *Rockwell*

Crewmen of a 12th BG B-25D nicknamed *Seven-Oh-Seven* arrive at their mount for yet another bombing mission in the MTO. Their living conditions in North Africa (note tent city in background) were less than desirable. *USAF via Jeff Ethell*

ment squadrons, the 12th BG made its first attack on 14 August 1942.

By early 1943, another four bombardment groups—the 310th, 319th, 321st, and 340th—had entered into combat in the MTO. One of these groups however—the 319th—operated B-26s for a time before they were replaced with B-25s. In fact, its B-26s were not replaced with B-25s until late 1944.

The B-25D (41-29707) nicknamed *Seven-Oh-Seven* was forced to make a wheels-up landing due to the loss of its hydraulic system via enemy gunfire. As can be seen, all six crewmen survived the ordeal. *USAF via Rockwell*

Even when much heavier damage than this had been dealt to B-25s in combat, they made it back to home base more often than not. This B-25J returned home even though its tail turret and tail gunner are gone. *Rockwell*

Since the B-26 needed larger airfields than the B-25, the B-26 operated from air bases in England while the USAAF B-25 did not. Although the B-25's rival had more powerful engines and greater speed, it did not have the short field capability of the B-25. Therefore, better suited to the smaller air bases in the South Pacific and Southwest Pacific area, and in the MTO and CBI theaters, the B-25 prevailed. The reason the 319th BS was able to keep its B-26s for so long was that it operated from Tafarouri Airdrome at Oran, Algeria, which was a large base. The reason it replaced its B-26s with B-25s in late 1944 was that its B-26s were all high-time aircraft and new Mitchells without any time were available.

The 12th, 310th, 319th, 321st, and 340th BGs were assigned to the Twelfth Air Force, XII Bomber Command. Like all other USAAF air forces and bomber commands the Twelfth Air Force contributed a great deal to the war effort. As follows, 57th Bombardment Wing historian John J. Sutay, for the fiftieth anniversary of the 57th BW Association, in its publication, *The B-25 over the Mediterranean*, wrote:

The 12th Air Force, which from D-Day in North Africa to V-Day in Italy, provided Allied ground forces with strategic and tactical support, was America's first invasion air force and the first to help attain a final victory.

From the onset the keynote of the 12th's support was its versatility. At the height of the North African campaign it was the world's largest single air force and remained that way until its heavy bombers [B-17s and B-24s] were separated and grouped under what became the Fifteenth Air Force.

If the axis didn't get you, mother nature did. When Mt. Vesuvius (now Vesuvio) erupted on 22 March 1944, the 340th BG was based at Pompeii, Italy. A number of its B-25 aircraft were either buried with ash and cinders from volcanic fallout or destroyed together. But with hard work and a move from Pompeii to Paestum, all salvageable 340th BG B-25s were back in action in three days. *Rockwell*

A lone B-25D of the 345th BG, 500th BS, the "Rough Raiders," banks right to continue the attack on the island below. Nicknamed "Pannell Job," this D (41-30024) mounted four .50-caliber machine guns in a solid nose (a field modification). Unfortunately, during a training flight on 11 June 1944, its pilot Lt. Ray Pannell and two other crewmen were killed when the airplane inexplicably dived into the ground from 5,000ft near Nadzab, New Guinea. *Rockwell*

A beautifully restored solid nose B-25J represents the 345th BG, the "Air Apaches," 498th BS, the "Falcons," with civil registration number N6020B. *Don Truax via Campbell Archives*

An odd-colored, shark-mouthed, glass nose B-25J sits out a lonely vigil at an unknown location (civil registration number N6013); no guns or gun turrets. *Don Truax via Campbell Archives*

A lone B-25 charges the Muroc *Maru* to practicing strafing and skip-bombing tactics for subsequent action against real Japanese shipping in the Pacific. *Rockwell*

After that fighters, fighter-bombers and night fighters, light and medium bombers of the 12th were used to blast the Luftwaffe [German Air Force] from the Mediterranean skies, isolate the ene-my by severing his lines of communication, and provide Allied ground units with close cooperation to carry out the three-fold purpose of a tactical air force.

In the 905 days the 12th Air Force was in combat, its planes flew 408,343 combat sorties [missions] and dropped more than 218,000 tons of bombs. Its fighters and bombers destroyed and damaged almost 5,000 enemy planes. In the last year of fighting alone, it destroyed and damaged almost 35,000 enemy motor vehicles, more than 25,000 railroad cars, and some 2,100 bridges.

It sunk 263 enemy ships and boats damaging 650 others. Its photo[graphic] reconnaissance squadrons turned out millions of prints for ground and air intelligence.

The 12th became the first air force in the world to be given full credit for the surrender of ground objectives when the Mediterranean Sea island of Pantelleria was occupied in June 1943, after devastating aerial bombardments had forced its surrender.

After losing the B-17s and B-24s with the organization of the 15th Air Force, the 12th AF struck blow after blow at enemy forces and installations with B-25 and B-26 medium bombers, and A-20 and A-26 light bombers. The Mitchells and Marauders were employed for their "pinpoint" precision, while the Havocs and Invaders were used as night intruders that permitted the enemy no respite even when darkness cloaked his movements.

The principal components of the Mediterranean Allied Air Force [MAAF] were made up of American, British, Brazilian, Canadian, South African, Polish, and French airmen. The 12th Air Force was commanded by some of the most famous airmen and tacticians in military history—USAAF Generals Carl A. Spaatz, John C. Cannon, Benjamin W. Chidlaw, and James H. Doolittle.

Good as the 12th AF was, though, it was just one air force out of at least nine others that employed the B-25. These are as follows: 4th AF, Far Western United States; 5th AF, Southwest Pacific; 7th AF, Central Pacific; 9th AF, France; 10th AF, India-Burma; 11th AF, Alaska; 13th AF, South Pacific; 14th AF, China; and 15th AF, Italy (locations are as of late 1945).

Moreover, the B-25 was used by at least fifteen medium-class bombardment groups: 1st Air Commando Group, 1st BG, 3rd BG, 12th BG, 17th BG, 22nd BG, 28th Composite Group, 38th BG, 41st BG, 42nd BG, 310th BG, 321st BG, 340th BG, 341st BG, and the 345th BG. Literally, the B-25 was everywhere. And by the end of 1943, it was being used for every possible mission: high-level, medium-level, and low-level bombardment; low-level strafing and skip bombing; medium- and high-level mapping and photographic reconnaissance; high-speed transportation; light attack bombardment and strafing; and as patrol bombardment (anti shipping) aircraft. What is more, each bombardment group had up to five squadrons. These are shown below:

| Bombardment Group | Bombardment Squadron | Comment |
| --- | --- | --- |
| 1st BG Group | 1st BS | Chinese-American Composite |
| | 2nd BS | |
| | 3rd BS | |
| | 4th BS | |
| 1st Air Commando Group | | Used twelve B-25H airplanes in 1944 |
| 3rd BG | 8th BS | |
| | 13th BS | |
| | 89th BS | Not to be confused with the 89th RS below |
| | 90th BS | |
| 12th BG | 81st BS "Butting Goats" | The 12th BG was nicknamed the "Earthquakers" |
| | 82nd BS "Bulldogs" | |
| | 83rd BS "Black Angels" | |
| | 434th BS "Cyclones" | |
| 17th BG | 34th BS "Thunderbirds" | |
| | 37th BS | |
| | 95th BS" Kicking Mules" | |
| | 89th RS | The 89th was a reconnaissance squadron attached to the 17th BG |
| 22nd BG | 2nd BS | |
| | 33rd BS | |
| | 408th BS | |
| 28th Composite Group | | Used B-25s of the 73rd, 77th, and 406th BSs |
| 38th BG | 69th BS | |
| | 70th BS | |
| | 405th BS | |
| | 822nd BS | |
| | 823rd BS | |
| 41st BG | 47th BS | |
| | 48th BS | |
| | 75th BS | |
| | 396th BS | |
| | 820th BS | |
| 42nd BG | 69th BS | |
| | 70th BS | |
| | 75th BS | |
| | 100th BS | |
| | 390th BS "Crusaders" | |
| 310th BG | 379th BS | |
| | 380th BS | |
| | 381st BS | |
| | 428th BS | |
| 319th BG | 437th BS | The 319th BG converted from B-26s to B-25s beginning on 5 October 1944 |
| | 438th BS | |
| | 439th BS | |
| | 440th BS | |
| 321st BG | 445th BS | |
| | 446th BS | |
| | 447th BS | |
| | 448th BS | |

| Bombardment Group | Bombardment Squadron | Comment |
| --- | --- | --- |
| 340th BG | 486th BS | |
| | 487th BS | |
| | 488th BS | |
| | 489th BS | |
| 341st BG | 11th BS | |
| | 22nd BS | |
| | 490th BS | |
| | 491st BS | |
| 345th BG | 498th BS "Falcons" | The 34th BG was nicknamed the "Air Apaches" |
| | 499th BS "Bats Outa' Hell" | |
| | 500th BS "Rough Raiders" | |
| | 501st BS "Black Panthers" | |
| 477th BG | 616th BS | The 477th BG was an all-black unit |
| | 617th BS | |
| | 618th BS | |
| | 619th BS | |

A brand-new B-25D runs up its engines at NAA's Kansas City plant just before its first man-ufacturers check flight prior to its delivery to the USAAF. *Rockwell*

Before VJ-Day, the B-25 was used by the US Army Air Forces, US Navy, US Marine Corps, US Coast Guard, and a number of allied and friendly countries. It proved to be a relatively fast bomber plane that was reliable and easy to fly. Maneuverable and agile, the Mitchell was an outstanding combat airplane. And with its ability to bomb targets with pinpoint accuracy, it demonstrated that it was a stable bombardment platform.

Mitchell bombers became immediately famous with the Halsey-Doolittle Raid. Some, like the Mitchell nicknamed *Bones*, were more famous than others.

### Bones

During a well-attended ceremony on 7 July 1944 at Inglewood, NAA president "Dutch" Kindleberger presented the 3,208th and last California-built Mitchell to Brig. Gen. Donald H. Stace, chief of the western procurement district of the USAAF. It was also the 1,000th and last production B-25H. As the ceremony proceeded, the hundreds of men and women who helped build it looked on with pride.

The Inglewood plant was changing over to exclusive production of P-51s and, after years of building B-25s, the employees felt emotional about Mitchell number 3,208. Under the circumstances, USAAF Commanding Gen. "Hap" Arnold granted special permission for the workers to inscribe their names on this final California-built Mitchell. Thus, from nose to tail, from top to bottom, the plane was blanketed with thousands of names, in all the colors of the spectrum. Names like Earl and Sue and Al and Blondie and Chuck were printed and scrawled over every inch of the surface, even on the rims of the landing gear wheels. And sometime during the autographing process, B-25H number 1,000 was nicknamed *Bones*.

Shortly afterward, this special airplane also known as Billy Mitchell 1000, was ferried to the Third Air Force processing station at Hunter Army Air Field, Savannah, Georgia. There, it became the center of attention on another vital World War II assembly line, where combat aircraft of all types were being prepared for overseas operations by trained USAAF crew members.

While *Bones* was going through its exhaustive checkup, the same thing was happening to the crew of five men assigned to take it into combat. At Hunter Field combat crews from various training bases, as well as gleaming new bombers from the factories, arrived daily to be blended into the mighty combination of battle-ready men and machines that fought and won World War II.

What the Third Air Force thought of the men who would fly *Bones* and all her sister planes against the enemy was evident from the inscription over the door of the combat crew center, focal point for personnel processing. The sign read: "Through these doors pass the best damn flyers in the world."

Through that same door passed the eager members of the *Bones* crew, fresh from a rigid course of training under simulated combat conditions at a medium-class bombardment base at Columbia, South Carolina.

These crew members were a cross section of the US Army Air Forces. The pilot, Second Lt. Robert B. Allen, was a civil engineer from Campbellton, Texas, who served with an aviation engineer company in the Southwest Pacific before he was sent back to the United States for flight training. The copilot, Second Lt. Kenneth L. Voight, of Red Rock, Texas, began his Army service with field artillery. Tail gunner Corp. Seymour Leon, Chicago, Illinois, was a theatrical agent. Corp. Wilmer C. Odom, of Stonewall, Mississippi, left premedical studies to enter the USAAF and became a flight engineer. Not long out of high school was the radio operator, Corp. William D. Downey, of Greensburgh, Pennsylvania. Lt. Voight doubled as navigator.

The five men moved through the final details of processing, impatient for their first look at the airplane they would fly in combat. Finally, with their baggage stenciled and weighed, they headed for the ramp where *Bones* stood in line, awaiting her crew.

"We've got a helluva lot of people rooting for us," said Lieutenant Allen, as he stared at the covering of signatures.

"Right, sir," agreed Corporal Leon. "We won't let 'em down."

The crew loaded their baggage on the plane and took up their positions. There followed a whine of the starters, a roar of the engines as they coughed to life, and *Bones* rumbled down the taxiway.

"Hunter tower from B-25. Request

take-off instruction, over," the pilot's voice sounded over the speaker in the control tower.

"Hunter tower to B-25. All clear. Take the air," came the reply.

*Bones* thundered down the runway and slipped into the air, another bomber of thousands processed for combat duty at Hunter Field, but the only one carrying the names of all the Rosies and Mikes and Bobs and Marthas and Georges who produced her.

Then on 30 November 1944, after its long distance ferry flight from the United States, *Bones* arrived at Karachi, India, in good condition. Assigned to the Tenth Air Force, 81st Bombardment Squadron (medium), 12th Bombardment Group, the airplane proceeded to show what she could do.

On 6 December, she attacked a bridge near Toungoo, Burma, with six 500lb general purpose bombs. On 7 December, she dropped twenty-two 100lb incendiaries on enemy installations at Taungtha, Burma. On 12 December, she let go a string of bombs on runways to an enemy air base at Thedaw, with "excellent results." And on 15 December, she attacked a bridge south of Toungoo and destroyed two spans of the bridge with six 500lb general purpose bombs.

This B-25G, nicknamed *Pride of the Yankees*, being readied for yet another mission. Ordnance men are cleaning the bore of its 75mm cannon. The two spent 75mm shell cases covering the barrels of its twin .50-caliber nose guns—to keep dirt out—is noteworthy. *F. C. Dickey via Ernest R. McDowell*

*Bones*, then, the last B-25 Mitchell to leave the assembly line of NAA's Inglewood plant, had begun to live up to all the expectations of the men and the women who had given it such a great send-off on 7 July 1944. As of 27 December 1944—some five and a half months later, still covered with signatures—the airplane had engaged the enemy five times with telling effect in the central Burma area.

In early 1945 Lieutenant Allen said, "*Bones* is a running fool. We love this ship; and we ought to, for she has brought us 15,000 miles without a complaint. She's temperamental...but we're on to all her tricks."

*Bones*, with large number forty-fives stenciled on the outboard sides of her vertical tails, sporting USAAF serial number 43-5104, proved that she meant business. Most unfortunately, her final disposition remains unknown.

Somewhere over Burma, a lone B-25H of the 1st Air Command heads home after delivering its payload as smoke rises from other targets already bombed by other B-25Hs of the 1st Air Commando. *Smithsonian*

## B-25 Training

B-25 training for pilots and copilots, bombardiers, radio operators, navigators, gunners, and cannoneers was thorough and extensive—especially for bombardiers, gunners, and cannoneers involved with the B-25s that had to strafe enemy land, sea, and air forces. The training that kept B-25 crews razor sharp was varied, and in a number of ways, unprecedented. One such training method involved a fake Japanese battleship—the Muroc *Maru*, made of

wood, and anchored in the giant dry lake next to Muroc AAF, California, in the Mojave Desert. This training was dubbed "Desert Finishing School." Below, from an article by Edward J. Ryan in the January-February 1945, issue of *Skyline*, a former NAA magazine, is how that B-25 training school worked.

The cluster of three B-25 Mitchells out in front suddenly banked sharply to the left and then leaped forward with their engines roaring at a new and higher pitch.

Our pilot straightened up and tightened his grip on the wheel. We banked and were away, following the leader. We'd been riding along in a relaxed alertness, but now the Mitchell crews tensed up.

This was it. Out of sight of the mountain was the target for today. A big sprawling dry lake bed and a large Japanese battleship waiting for those nice bombs

tucked up in neat racks inside the B-25s, sleek bellies, and those lovely rounds of 75mm artillery projectiles and 50cal machine gun bullets.

We'd been cruising along comfortably at 175mph. Now the air speed needle climbed steadily across the 200mph mark and up toward and over 300mph. We lost sight of the leaders briefly, but quickly we were abreast of them. Us and the other two on our wings, and the three other Mitchells in the nine-plane formation.

Quickly we regrouped in a broken line and the rugged terrain fell away behind us. Over the mountain and down over the dry lake swept our nine silver messengers of death. Setting the pace was a lone cannon-carrying Mitchell, its 75mm gun thrust out in eager anticipation.

Down, down, until it seemed we could almost reach out and pluck a handful of sage brush. The big air base sprawled out ahead. Then we were at the edge of the field cutting across its runways.

Supposed enemy fighters buzzed around us like angry hornets, weaving in and out of our formation from above and from the right and left. Our pilot, a veteran of fifty-five missions in the Pacific, didn't waver, oblivious to their presence. After all, the fighters were something the gunners had to worry about. That is unless one of them came in from the front, in front of our plane's two package guns on either side of the fuselage. Then our pilot would do a little gunning on his own.

We turned away from the field, no longer brushing the ground but still plenty low. Then like homing pigeons, we headed for the big Jap[anese] cruiser, coming in broadside in a steep dive, then leveling off and cutting sharply up and over its largest mast.

After our practice run on the Jap[anese] cruiser—no one ever did actually fire live rounds at it; it wasn't to be destroyed—we had one more target to deal with. We went back to treetop level for this one. Again we raced across the dry lake. Our bomb bay doors snapped open and our four package .50cals began to chatter.

The Mitchell with its flying artillery piece let go a 75mm round, and the center of the target disintegrated. Then bombs started falling from the bellies of our planes. We lost sight of them before they hit the simulated ground target.

The machine guns and cannon were still firing as we departed the target area. We could look back at the target, we could see what was left of the objective. Bull's-eye!

This finishing school, one of many for B-25 crewmen, was located in Hawaii, where its operations required 2,500 base, service, and instructor personnel and doubled the aircraft requirements for the Pacific area, since aircraft were in demand for both combat and training. It also drained off a lot of aviation gasoline from the islands' supply,

Off New Hanover Island on 16 February 1944, a 345th BG B-25 bombs a Japanese ship (note bomb in mid-air). *Smithsonian*

and used 200,000lb of practice bombs and 600,000 rounds of ammunition each month.

By moving the school to Muroc AAF, the USAAF conserved shipping monies vital to eventual victory over Japan and did away with one maintenance problem in the Pacific where ground crews were swamped with keeping Mitchells and other aircraft operational in the forward areas.

It was the Fourth Air Force that trained the crews of the B-25 and other aircraft in theater combat tactics on the US West Coast. Veterans of the Pacific air war were the instructors.

As a matter of interest, the Muroc *Maru* was assembled out of wood and

chicken wire at a cost of $30,000. Its price tag was one reason why it was not to be destroyed. It remained intact at Muroc-cum-Edwards until 1950. Having become a safety hazard for the multitude of aircraft being tested there, the order came for its removal. Though off limits, it must have been a real temptation to plant a practice bomb right in the middle of the Japanese cruiser sailing across Rogers Dry Lake (as it is called today).

*Chapter 5*

# Voices from the Past

During some forty-four months of combat in World War II—from 11 December 1941 to 14 August 1945 for the United States, its numerous Allies, and friends—a Bombardment Group (Medium) that was equipped with the North American B-25 Mitchell ordinarily had three Bombardment Squadrons (Medium) and one Photographic Reconnaissance or Mapping Squadron (Medium) with a total allotment of sixty-four airplanes. That is, sixteen for each squadron.

For example, the 12th BG, the "Earthquakers," had four sixteen-plane squadrons: the 81st BS, the "Butting Goats"; the 82nd BS, the "Bulldogs"; the 83rd BS, the "Black Angels"; and the 434th BS (formerly the 94th Reconnaissance Squadron), the "Cyclones."

Most B-25-equipped BGs, BSs, and RSs had the capitalized word Medium in parenthesis after BG, BS, and RS to indicate that their B-25 airplanes were medium-class bombardment and reconnaissance aircraft; thus 12th BG (Medium), 81st BS (Medium), and so on.

The BGs that were outfitted with the B-25 airplanes were under the command of a bombardment wing (BW) which, in turn, was under the command of an air force (AF). As the various BGs moved around during the war they were often placed under the commands of different BWs and AFs. Using the 12th BG as one example again, when the war ended, it was under the command of the 57th BW, which was under the command of the Tenth Air Force.

## Firsthand Accounts

The 12th BG, as well as numerous other BGs, operated thousands of B-25 airplanes, produced thousands of crewmen, and generated dozens of squadrons. Based around the world, literally in all theaters of operations, these patriotic crewmen put forth their maximum efforts for nearly four years of all-out combat. Some of their personal experiences of that hellish time follow.

## Douglas W. "Doug" Spawn, Lt. Col. USAF (Retired)
### 12th BG—the "Earthquakers," 82nd BS—the "Bulldogs"

"My first contact with the B-25 was in May 1941. I flew as copilot on a flight across the state of Washington to McChord Field, Tacoma, from Felts Field, Spokane. The plane was one of the very early B-25s with the straight [unbroken dihedral] wing. We flew through some severe weather over the Cascade mountains [separating eastern and western Washington] with zero flying problems. The pilot was very impressed with its flying characteristics as was I. I flew again in the same type of airplane [straight wing] as copilot on a trip to Arizona and California in June 1941. I did make several landings and noticed how stable the airplane was.

"I checked out as first pilot in the B-25 in January 1942 at McChord Field where they had twelve to fourteen B-25s assigned to us. We flew these to Esler Field in Louisiana in February 1942 with no mishaps. At Esler, our group [12th BG] was equipped fully with sixty-four B-25C and B-25D airplanes.

"After a thirty-day temporary duty assignment to Stockton, California, in May and June 1942 for coastal defense (remember the Battle of Midway?), we returned to Esler and received our combat orders for overseas deployment. We had been equipped with brand new pink [mauve] B-25Cs and B-25Ds. We then knew our destination: Africa!

"In late July 1942, we left Esler and ended up in Deversoir, Egypt, in early August. Two of our squadrons were stationed in Ismailia, Egypt, some fifteen miles to the north of our two squadrons. Every airplane in our group arrived safely, a record I doubt many other groups could claim. We flew overloaded planes through tropical weather fronts and landed on short runways—sometimes in severe adverse weather. The airplane was dependable! I feathered many pro-

Twelfth Air Force ordnance men roll 1,000lb bombs toward the B-25 they are preparing for battle. For the most part, this type of bomb was used to knock out German roads and rail lines in Italy; one such bomb was able to block either. *USAF*

Lt. Col. Doug Spawn. *USAF*

pellers for maintenance checks and single engine flight was absolutely no problem; it was done with landing gear down, flaps extended, bomb bay doors open, and under many other maneuvering conditions. When the airplane stalled, it fell straight through without falling off on either wing tip. Turns were made into the dead engine with complete stability. It truly was a pilot friendly airplane.

"In combat the B-25 proved its worth many, many times over. We flew through desert dust storms and even mountain snowstorms in Northern Algeria. The airplane was also able to take severe punishment from enemy flak [antiaircraft artillery fire] and fighter gunfire. In most cases the aircraft were able to return to home base. On one mission in particular my airplane received more than 100 flak holes, both in the wings and fuselage. It was patched up and two days later it was in the air again dropping bombs on the enemy.

"Maintenance-wise, our aircraft remained in good shape, and they were always ready for maximum effort. Maintenance crews improvised constantly to keep them flying and fighting.

"The first problem I encountered in a combat situation was desert sand and dust in the carburetor air filters. The sand and dust took its toll on the engines, especially if we removed the air filters for high altitude operations up to 17,000 ft. Our maintenance personnel took special care of those filters!

"The second problem was the B-25's original engine exhaust pipes [stacks]. Each engine having only one large diameter exhaust pipe. On a clear night—and there were many—ground gunners and fighter pilots could easily see the exhaust gases (blue and/or orange in color against the nighttime skies) anywhere from 8,000 to 10,000ft, which were our normal operating altitudes. We complained to higher authority about this deadly vulnerability. After we lost four out of ten B-25s on the night of 14 September 1942, including the commander of our bomb group [Lt. Col. Charles G. Goodrich] and his crew, we were ordered to do no more night missions until the exhaust pipe problem was solved. It was solved by North American Aviation engineers with the use of "finger-type" exhaust pipes—one for each of the fourteen cylinders per engine. Then we resumed night operations.

"Through the years 1943, 1944, and 1945, after I returned to the United States, I continued to fly the B-25 as supervisor of flying training at Morris Field in North Carolina. We flew thousands of hours to train Douglas A-20 Havoc pilots. Student pilots experienced very few problems as they first transitioned into the Mitchell and then into the Havoc. Overwhelmingly, our students liked the B-25. They found it to be an excellent transition airplane—very stable, and trouble free.

"Outside of combat, the only fatal accident I can recall was a B-25D which crashed near Yoakum, Texas, in 1942 before I went to Egypt. The entire crew was killed. The pilot was a very dear friend. In fact, he was my best man at my wedding at the McChord Field chapel in January 1942. After the crash investigation, the cause was believed to be a malfunction in the automatic flight control system which, at the time, was a relatively new feature in the B-25.

"All in all, I feel, there was no better combat training than I received, or a purer combat airplane that I flew, than the B-25. It operated in all theaters of operations—even over heavily defended enemy nations, and returned their crews to home base with a very low accident rate that was second to no other World War II combat airplane."

## Mission to Rabaul, 18 October 1943, by Victor W. "Vic"Tatelman, Lt. Col. USAF (Retired)
345th BG—the "Air Apaches," 499th BS—the "Bats Outa' Hell"

"First some background: Rabaul, south of Truk on the north end of New Britain, was the main base of the Japanese forces in the Southwest Pacific area. All of the enemy forces on New Guinea were supplied from Rabaul; also, the Japanese fighter and bomber strength was concentrated in that area. Simpson Harbor, a major Naval base at Rabaul, was the permanent port for two cruisers, two destroyers, and several corvettes. Thus, without question, Rabaul was a prime target of the US Army Air Forces.

"From the summer of 1942 to the summer of 1943, Rabaul had been hit more or less regularly by B-17s of the 19th Bombardment Group and by B-26s of the 22nd BG, especially during the Allied operations against Guadalcanal and the Southern Solomons, but the missions never contained more than a dozen airplanes and the damage was never extensive. Aerial reconnaissance invariably reported over 100 combat-ready Japanese aircraft in the Rabaul area.

"The primary mission of the Fifth Air Force in the New Guinea campaign was to destroy the Japanese Air Forces in the Southwest Pacific area, especially the bomber force at Rabaul, which could have hindered the Allied advance along the north of New Guinea. By the late summer of 1943, Rabaul was within range of the B-25s of the Fifth AF, as Dobodura on the north coast of New Guinea had been secured and staging airfields had been built. The mission of 18 October 1943 was designed to destroy the enemy air forces at Rabaul.

"The Strike Plan: With fighter cover, two B-24 BGps would attack in the ear-

ly morning, simulating an attack on Rabaul Township, to draw the Japanese fighters up to intercept the B-24s. Then the B-24s would turn and make their bomb runs on all but two airstrips, destroying any aircraft (particularly bombers in revetments adjacent to the strips), pockmarking the runways, and forcing the returning Japanese fighters to land on the two undamaged strips at Rapopo and Tobera. Two groups of B-25s, the 38th and 345th, would then attack those two airstrips, hopefully catching the refueling enemy planes on the ground along with the bombers that were based there. According to intelligence reports on 16 October, total aircraft strength in the area was eighty-nine fighters, sixty-five medium-class bombers and twenty-one light class bombers.

"On 17 October thirty-six B-25s of the 345th Bombardment Group (Medium) left Port Moresby on the southern coast of New Guinea; the 499th Bombardment Squadron (Medium), my squadron, from Fourteen Mile strip. Arriving at Dobodura on the north coast of New Guinea in the middle of a red alert, the planes held off from landing for about an hour, finally landing at Strip Fifteen at about 1100 hours.

"The 345th BGp was led by deputy group commander Lt. Col. Clinton U. True in the lead squadron, the 498th

BSq; followed by the 501st BSq in the number two position in the group formation, the 499th BSq in the number three position, and the 500th BSq in the number four position.

"My squadron, the 499th BSq, had three flights of three B-25s. The 499th was comprised of:

"Flight One—Capt. Orin N. Loverin (squadron leader), Lt. Kenneth D. McClure, and Lt. Richard Baker.

"Flight Two—Lt. George L. Cooper, Lt. William N. Parke, and Lt. William W. Cabell.

"Flight Three—Capt. Julian B. Baird (squadron commanding officer), Lt. Victor W. Tatelman (yours truly), and Lt. Phillip Gath.

"Mission to Rabaul: Rabaul was indeed the fortress of the Japanese Air Forces in the Southwest Pacific area. Everyone knew that we would be flying into the jaws of hell when we finally attacked it.

"When we staged at Dobodura for the mission, we slept on strange uncomfortable cots without air mattresses. The hot, muggy New Guinea night of 17 October was especially bad even for the tropics. It was after 0300 hours and sleep was elusive. I had just fallen asleep when the operations clerk nudged me

Vic Tatelman's B-25C-1-NA, *Dirty Dora*. A high-time plane, *Dirty Dora* flew eighty combat missions before it was retired. *Vic Tatelman Collection via Jeff Ethell*

through my mosquito netting. The thought of Rabaul brought on a cold sweat as we dressed in silence. Captain Baird and I walked down to the mess tent; stomachs too tight for food—just coffee—then on to the briefing.

"When the briefing map is uncovered the fear becomes living, tangible, gnawing—Rabaul! First, just a minimum briefing—formation position, flight leaders, Navy blinker letter, and call signs. Next came the report by the intelligence officer, Joe Stephens, an Australian liaison officer: 'When you go down, aahh, I mean *if* you go down, make your way to this location,' and he points to a location of the map of New Britain. Then, our takeoff sequence was given and we 'hacked' our watches to synchronize our time.

"Now the final and detailed briefing. The lines and positions on the chart get translated into names and times, points and sequences. I glance at my copilot, Willie Graham; he's taking notes and looking grim. I wink and get a weak smile in return. I think back to our training together, and the formation of 499th BSq crew. He's a good copilot, invariably ready at the precise moment for his part of the joint effort.

"Captain Loverin leads the 499th take off at 1000 hours and assembles our squadron over the airstrip; Captain Baird leads our flight. I'm on his right wing; Lieutenant Gath on his left wing. Baird is a damn good flight leader; his instructions and his guidance are precise. Gath and I are both comfortable and confident in his precision flying ability.

"The 345th BGp assembles over Oro Bay and heads for the target at an altitude of 2,000ft. Two 38th BGp squadrons join us over the Buna wreck along with three squadrons of P-38 fighters. The assembled formation now heads for Kabanga Bay, the initial point of attack.

"Shortly after leaving Dobodura, the concentration of clouds begins to increase and after forty-five minutes the front ahead appears to be solid up to 12,000ft. Our group leader, Colonel True, looks for a hole, finds none, and heads into the turbulent blackness. The pilot tension in one plane during IFR [instrument flight rules] is considerable, but to have fifty aircraft on instruments in the same area.... Captain Baird turns on his blue formation lights—it helps a little. Gath and I snuggle close; cannot lose him in this weather; I'm practically in *his* cockpit! Willie helps on the wheel; he and I are beginning to think alike.

"There is a break in the clouds; we can see the formation is moving down to go through on the deck. The fighter cover is gone. Then the radio command from base to abort the mission and return to Dobodura. Colonel True maintains his heading; he has decided to continue the mission unescorted. We move down to 100ft; it appears no one was lost in the weather.

"The closer we get to the target the more the fear builds up. Everybody feels it, but it's not mentioned. Talk is clipped, reduced to monosyllables; more so since the fighter cover is gone. The weather must have turned them back; I wonder if True knows they're gone. I can't believe he's taking the Group to Rabaul unescorted!

"Flying to the target we're busy holding formation, loading and testing guns, reviewing the attack plan, navigating, recognizing ground features, and all the time, the fear mounts. When the target area is sighted, the fear drops away and is replaced by calm concentration. I know exactly what I'm doing, and what I'm assigned to do. The crew is sharp and alert; their familiar tasks and duties are second nature. I have no concern about their coming performance; our crew is a team, we rely and believe in our own abilities and in each other.

"As we cross the coast of New Britain the 38th BG leaves us for their targets. Colonel True leads our Group to a point about 10 miles south of Rapopo airstrip where we start our right turn into our bomb run. Since the 498th and 501st BSqds preceded the 499th BSqd over the target, and in order to let them clear the area, Captain Loverin leads the 499th in a 360-degree circle just south of the target, then over the airstrip from south to north. Antiaircraft artillery [AAA] batteries cover both ends of the strip as well as two on either side of the strip. Ack ack is heavy. But it is not accurate.

"As we approach the target there is no sound except for the drone of two engines and occasional directions on the command radio. Then the targets appear: a AAA battery, an airplane in a revetment, a building. The concentration is intense; fire the nose guns, release the bombs. Even with all the noise, smoke, and gun chatter, the movements and actions of the crew are very smooth. With the violent reaction of the nose guns, however, the airplane shudders. The engines are at meto [medium take-off] power, bombs are exploding, the confusion of flying through smoke and black AAA puffs; aiming at targets on the ground, keeping one eye on Captain Baird—can't let him get in our line of fire—it all blends, almost in slow motion. Willie has one hand lightly on the wheel, feet on the rudders—if I am hit, he must fly imme-

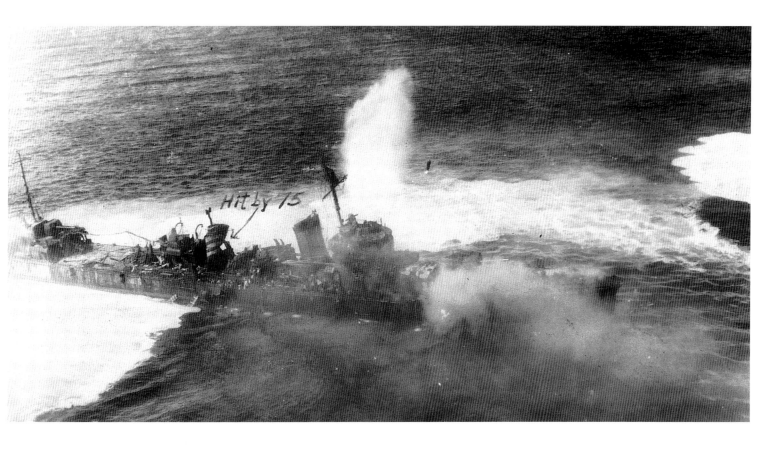

Hit by 75

Two views of the Japanese destroyer bombed by a new 75mm cannon-equipped B-25G. *Rockwell*

diately—so close to the ground, so fast, the split second to grab the wheel would be fatal if he is not already on it.

"The west side of Rapopo strip is covered by dense smoke from the bombed and strafed planes that had been attacked by the 498th and 501st BSqds ahead of us. The targets are mostly obscured by the smoke. But this also limits the effectiveness of the Japanese AAA batteries, giving us some protection. The inaccuracy of the Japanese gunners may be due to our surprise raid or to their lack of practice. Only one other low-level attack had ever been launched against Rabaul.

"Leaving Rapopo airstrip and crossing the beach we notice several ships in the bay, especially one that looks like a ferry boat directly in our line of flight. All three B-25s in our flight strafe the boat, observing direct hits, and people diving and/or falling into the water. We broke right and the three airplanes of our flight joined up rapidly. But it is some time before our flight joins up

Carl R. Wilder (left) with the crew of the second B-25B to launch from the USS *Hornet* on 18 April 1942. *USAF*

with Loverin and the rest of the 499th BSqd. Not one 499th BSqd airplane had been lost over the target, but the fun is about to begin.

"When the first B-25s of the 498th, 500th, and 501st BSsqs came off their targets they are met with swarms of Mitsubishi A6M3 "Zekes"—Japanese carrier-based fighters. Luckily for the 499th BSqd, the first three squadrons had attracted most of the fighters. It was always a dilemma for the pilots: Do I expend all the ammunition for the nose guns over the target, or do I conserve some for a possible head-on pass by a fighter? Off Cape Gazelle the 499th BSqd is jumped by fifteen Zekes. A total of twenty-one passes are made; most break off before coming into range. Ten passes come within range and three Zekes are shot down by our gunners in Flights One and Two. All nine planes of the 499th BSqd returned to Dobodura safely.

90

"Lt. Gen. George C. Kenney's dilemma: The 345th BGp had a tough mission to Wewak on 16 October 1943. Two days later, Colonel True had led thirty-three planes to attack Rabaul. The B-24s tried to work around the weather on 18 October, but finally aborted the mission. The P-38 fighters turned their formation around and headed for home when they too hit the weather.

"At this point radio operators in most planes received a message from headquarters canceling the mission. Everyone in the 345th BGp watched in surprise as Colonel True continued toward Rabaul. Colonel True later claimed his radio operator never received the message to abort the mission.

"Back at Dobodura, Col. Frederic Smith at 1st Air Task Force Headquarters didn't believe the story and was ready to nail Colonel True for disobeying orders to cancel the Rabaul raid.

"Three days later Colonel True was ordered to Brisbane to report to General Kenney, commander of the Fifth AF. True reported twenty-two kills of Japanese fighter planes with five probables by the 345th BGp; this did not include five

that flew into the water. Many more were destroyed on the ground by strafing and parafrags [parachute-retarded fragmentation bombs]. Two planes of the Group had to ditch; two men of those crews were saved.

"He reported his story about not receiving the radio message. General Kenney didn't believe him any more than most of his pilots had, but a court-martial didn't seem appropriate. After consulting Maj. Gen. Ennis C. Whitehead, in charge of the Fifth AF's advance echelon in New Guinea, General Kenney decided the Distinguished Service Cross, the nation's second highest award for valor, was more in line.

"Later Colonel True read headlines in Brisbane newspapers: 'MacArthur using daring new tactics, sends B-25s over Rabaul unescorted.' Colonel True reasoned, 'If they are going to try me now, I'll say it was Mac's idea."

### Dirty Dora

Vic Tatelman (see above) flew one of the more famed Mitchell airplanes—NA-82 B-25C-1-NA (41-12971) nicknamed *Dirty Dora*. Before it was declared war weary on 30 August 1944, *Dirty Dora* had flown at least 175 combat missions; it might have flown more than 180 but this has not been confirmed. Below, from the November-December 1944 issue of *Skyline*, a magazine formerly published by NAA for its management, an anonymous Fifth Air Force captain tells its story:

"The telephone jangled at Group Operations (38th BG) and a voice at the other end of the Command wire said quietly but with a hint of excitement, 'Get the boys ready for a briefing. . . . We are going to sink the whole Jap [anese] fleet.'

"Within a few moments, the leisurely pace of life in the tropics was galvanized into the action of mad efficiency that only the prospect of an immediate encounter with the enemy could produce. The same thing happened throughout the entire Fifth Air Force.

"The briefing was elaborate, telling the number of enemy ships, their approximate position, and the new methods of skip bombing attack. But the boys were too excited to sit and listen. They fidgeted and shifted uneasily in their seats and almost unconsciously soaked up the details of the attack. Each

*Bones,* the 1,000th and last B-25H produced at NAA's Inglewood plant (USAAF serial number 43-5104). In fact it was the last California-built Mitchell. Covered with the autographs of the men and women who built her, *Bones* became one of fifteen other B-25s of the 81st BS, 12th BG and served until VJ-Day without ever receiving a standard paint job. *Rockwell*

To honor NAA technical representative Jack Fox (shown), this field-modified B-25G was nicknamed *Lil' Fox*. The 75mm cannon was nicknamed *Big Dick*, and as this rare untouched photograph proves, the airplane was actually called B*ig Dick and Lil' Fox*. Rockwell

pilot was thinking to himself, 'I'm going to get one of those damned Jap[anese] ships!'

"It seemed only a few hours later that a slim, well-built and sandy-haired pilot of a Billy Mitchell was peering out over the Bismarck Sea [north of New Guinea and New Britain]. Below, there was nothing save the shimmering reflection of the multicolored tropical waters. As he looked out over his ship, its name caught his eye. He half-smiled, recalling the happenstance of that name.

"'Good old Dora,' thought the pilot. A call from the flight leader woke him from his reverie: 'There's the Jap[anese] fleet. Let's give them hell, men.'

"You may find many a well-written account of how the enemy fleet was bat-

tered, and how it finally turned tail and fled with its remnants. *Dirty Dora* had embarked on a glorious career with three Jap[anese] warships destroyed and not a single scratch on her skin.

"As the months passed, *Dirty Dora* piled up mission after mission until, in August of 1943, she had almost fifty combat missions and still was good as new.

"On a fateful day in August 1943, she flew as one of those strafers who descended so unexpectedly upon Wewak [on the north coast of New Guinea] and caught most of the Jap[anese] planes on the ground. The enemy knew that Wewak was out of range of the B-25s from Port Moresby (on the south coast of New Guinea; at that time the closest United States base), but they had not considered the American capacity for doing the impossible. Even before this day, they had learned to fear the plane that was at one time only a medium bomber; but now, too, a low-level strafer. They could now get used to the idea of bombs *and* bullets from treetop level—at the same time.

"With almost sixty missions to her credit, *Dirty Dora* was transferred to another Group [the 345th BG] that had been overseas only a few months [on 7 August 1943]. It seemed to those who had known her so well that she was like an old race horse ready to be turned out into the pasture for the rest of her days.

"No one dreamed that her career had hardly begun.

"But the 'Bats Outa' Hell' squadron [the 499th BS] of the 'Air Apaches' Group [the 345th BG] reconditioned her and gave her a coat of paint. On 18 October 1943, *Dirty Dora* again left Port Moresby for the first raid on Rabaul [see above] on the north coast of New Britain, which was just as disastrous for the enemy as the one on Wewak. On the next mission to Wewak, a Zeke slipped in between the fighter escort and trained his guns on *Dirty Dora*. Machine gun bullets tore into her fuselage and knocked out the hydraulic system. It would have been the end of *Dirty Dora* had not the upper turret gunner caught the Zeke in his gun[s] sight. A burst from the twin fifties [two .50cal machine guns] and there was no Zeke.

"It was a small matter to make the necessary repairs and put the veteran back into the Battle for New Guinea.

"There was another mission to Wewak, another to Rabaul, and then numerous missions to Cape Gloucester, the Admiralty Islands, Hansa Bay, Alexishafen, Saidor, Hollandia, Wake Island, Biak Island, and the Molucca Islands.

"The story of *Dirty Dora* is, actually, a story without a hero. While tens of thousands of brave Americans are helping to win the war by their daring exploits, let us not forget that the enemy, too, are brave and daring men. The point of this story lies in the superiority of American weapons and ingenuity.

"Salute, then, our *Dirty Dora* and the thousands of aircraft like her that are helping us to win our war for freedom. There are other planes with more missions, with more destroyed ships painted on their sides, with more Jap[anese] airplanes scratched on their roster, but none that has served more faithfully. Salute, also, the people back home who are giving us the material for incontestable aerial superiority.

"As an astute observer once said, 'It is a very fine thing to die for one's country, but it is much more satisfying to make the enemy die for his.' That sums up the virtues of *Dirty Dora*."

*Note:* In addition to the numerous combat missions flown by *Dirty Dora*, she is also credited with the downing of four Japanese airplanes—a Zeke, an Oscar, and two undocumented others; she also accounted for three ships sunk.

### Joseph C. "Joe" Cotton, Jr., Lt. Col., USAF (Retired)
### 3rd Attack Group, 13th Attack Squadron

"Thinking about experiences that occurred more than fifty years ago always brings up the question: Which part is fact and which part is fiction, if any? I will try to stay with the facts as far as my memory will permit.

"To begin, I flew the Douglas A-20 Havoc more than I flew the North American B-25 Mitchell. And most of my time with the latter was as a copilot. I finished flying school in Class 43-F at Columbus, Mississippi. At that time the USAAF evidently was in great need of Boeing B-17 Flying Fortress and Consolidated B-24 Liberator pilots because as graduation time approached I was called in several times to review my choice of combat aircraft. I had selected the B-25 and they pressed hard for me to change

my choice to either the B-17 or B-24. I stayed with the B-25, and even though I later flew the A-20 more, I was never sorry about my decision. Simply put, it was the best-looking airplane I had ever seen.

"I guess I fell in love with the B-25 while in primary flying school at Arcadia, Florida. One day a B-25 landed on the no-runway grass field at Carlstrom Field at Arcadia and we had a chance to look it over and to speculate on how its pilot was going to get it off the ground

In one of the most successful attacks in World War II, thirty-six B-25s scored direct hits to leave the German battleship *Strasbourg* listing in addition to sinking a submarine and leaving another on its side; it also bombed a cruiser. These warships had been docked in Toulon Harbor. *USAF*

again from a field designed for Stearman PT-17 biplanes. We soon found out.

"The pilot finished his business at Carlstrom Field, walked out, looked at

In "Operation Uppercut," Tenth Air Force B-25s pounded coastal gun positions on the southern coast of France to soften up Axis defenses for the ground troops that invaded southern France on 15 August 1944; the operation, as far as B-25s were concerned, began thirteen days earlier. A B-25J is shown. *USAF*

the windsock, crawled into the B-25, started his engines, lined up into the wind, ran up the engines, dropped flaps and took off with room to spare. That left me and a bunch of other cadets standing with our mouths open in astonishment.

"Following graduation, I received orders that sent me to B-25 training at Columbia, South Carolina. I was assigned to a training squadron whose commanding officer was Capt. Dean Davenport, one of Doolittle's copilots on the Tokyo raid (Dean Davenport was the copilot of the fifth B-25B to launch from the *Hornet*; it was piloted by Ted W. Lawson). I was soon assigned to a group of B-25 copilots. All pilots were assigned as copilots on the B-25, to fly with First

Pilots as schedules demanded. This arrangement allowed new pilots to gain useful experience with the advantage of veteran pilot supervision and advice.

"In September 1943, my training was completed. We shipped to California by train and from there by air to Australia. We eventually arrived at Dobodura, New Guinea, and then we were assigned to the 3rd Attack Group, 13th Attack Squadron.

"Mission: Ground Support of Landing Forces at Cape Gloucester, New Britain, on 26 December 1943. The charge of quarters wakened the flight crews scheduled to fly a 4:30a.m. After dressing in the dark, a quick breakfast of powdered eggs, bacon, toast and coffee, the crews were loaded on trucks to go to the operations shack at the airstrip for briefing.

"Weather was predicted to be marginal with a low ceiling over Dobodura, but probably clear at the rendezvous area off Finschaven. We were to assemble and orbit over the Bismarck Sea until our services were needed.

"Capt. Charles Hewes and I preflighted our B-25, which of course had already been checked out by the crew chief and the line crew. The B-25 we were to fly was a modified 'D' model with nose and package guns giving the airplane a capacity of over 3,000 rounds of .50cal machine gun ammunition. It also was loaded with six 500lb demolition bombs.

"Earlier 1943, the B-25 strafers as originally modified by Col. Pappy Gunn, had played a major part in what came to be called 'The Battle of the Bismarck Sea,' when the Japanese tried to send a convoy of warships and troop ships to reinforce their forces at Lae, New Guinea. Many experienced Japanese troops, shops, and supplies were lost in the heavy air and sea battle that ensued.

"Back to our mission, using a flashlight the safety pins were pulled from the bomb fuses, counted and turned over to the crew chief. Our crew consisted of the pilot, copilot, navigator-bombardier, radio man, and two gunners.

We climbed aboard and settled into our assigned areas to wait for start engines time.

"At 4:30 a.m. the whine of the inertial starters on the B-25's twoR-2600 engines was heard as twelve Mitchells were fired up. After a brief warm-up the lead plane left the hardstand and taxied to the end of the strip, followed by eleven others.

"Take-off was scheduled at one-minute intervals, an unusually long interval time, designed to give the airplane taking off enough time to get out of the way of the next one as it climbed straight out toward the rendezvous point of Finschaven. No attempt to join up in a formation was to be made due to instrument takeoff conditions in darkness with the low ceiling over Dobodura.

"When our turn came Captain Hewes released the brakes and rolled the B-25 out of the hardstand area. He then lined up with the runway, ran up the engines and checked for any mag(neto) drop. This was followed by a brief run-up to near full power.

"All things checked, the gyro compass was set to zero degrees, and the flaps were lowered fifteen degrees. When hack time arrived he applied full throttle and fixed his eyes on the gauges.

"As copilot, I evened up the manifold pressure on the two engines at 40in of mercury and then stared into the distance ahead as far as our landing lights would allow.

"We lifted off, and after a slight delay to make sure we were airborne, Captain Hewes gave his wheels-up signal and I pulled the gear lever to the up position. After another few seconds he signaled to start raising the flaps.

"Five minutes later at 2,000ft the gyro compass, still set on zero, was reset to magnetic compass reading and we turned on course for Finschaven. We continued climbing, leveled off at 7,000ft, and settled down to cruise speed.

"As daylight slowly displaced the darkness we began to look around to see if we could spot any other aircraft but failed to see any until we approached the rendezvous area off Finschaven.

"As Captain. Hewes circled to the left our squadron leader fired an occasional red flare for identification. Slowly but surely individual B-25s joined for-mation, and when all twelve were in place, we flew north to orbit just west of Amboi island where we observed US naval warships of the landing force engaged in shelling Japanese shore positions on Cape Gloucester.

"Simultaneously, US naval landing boats were being loaded with our troops from the transport ships. Still, the shelling continued, and from above, B-24s were dropping their bombs on the target area. It was getting hectic.

"We continued to circle as the landing boats headed for shore. As they approached the beach the warships ceased their fire, the B-24s stopped their bombing, and the troops started unloading under fire from the Japanese.

"A few minutes later ground control located on one of the US naval destroyers called for our squadron to make strafing and bombing passes inland from the landing beach. After we lowered our altitude to 500ft, the eight forward-firing .50cal machine guns on each of our B-25s (four in the nose and four in the packages) seemed to put up a solid wall of bullets as each flight of three headed into the target area.

"Like the others, we released our six 500lb bombs; we hit pillboxes and trenches that came into view uphill from the beach. As usual it was difficult to assess damage done to these kinds of targets. I guess it is possible to assume that the Japanese kept their heads down under the hail of bullets provided by twelve B-25s. Not to mention the 500lb bombs we were unloading all over the area.

"We reassembled offshore past the area of US naval ship operations and after circling a few times ground control asked for another strafing and bombing pass on the Japanese positions. Most of our bombs were gone but quite a bit of .50cal machine gun ammunition was still available. On our second pass we did expend the remainder of that.

"Once more we reassembled offshore. Ground control, knowing we were out of bullets and bombs, released us to return to base. We flew in formation back to our airstrip at Dobodura and landed. Flight time: three hours, five minutes.

"Later that afternoon we received a message from the US naval Task Force commander commending the group for a job well done.

## Lil' Fox

The first 75mm cannon-equipped airplanes to see action in the Southwest Pacific were factory-fresh B-25Gs assigned to the Fifth Air Force; they had begun arriving in July 1943. They were immediately put into action against Japanese troops, air bases, and shipping. Many other cannon-equipped B-25Gs, and subsequently, B-25Hs soon appeared throughout the region. One such airplane, an early B-25G, was nick-named Lil' Fox for Jack Fox—the NAA technical representative who was most instrumental in the development of the cannon-armed B-25G/H aircraft.

## Anonymous NAA Technical Representative

After these 75mm cannon-carrying aircraft went into action, an anonymous NAA technical representative reported the following.

"In consecutive combat sorties [missions] against enemy shipping and troop concentrations the big gun had fired 180 75mm rounds in a very short time. The most spectacular mission was the one off Cape Gloucester, New Britain, when Larry York, another NAA technical representative told me of one particular B-25 attack on a very large Japanese destroyer.

"This large destroyer, and a smaller one, were hit by a lone 75mm cannon-armed B-25G and several B-25C and B-25D airplanes, without assistance of either fighters or other bombers. Skip bombing disabled the large destroyer, and stopped it, off New Britain—one of the large islands of the Netherlands East Indies.

"The pilot of the lone B-25G was struck by shrapnel on one of the strafing runs, but he was not critically wounded. Seven 75mm projectiles were fired into the large destroyer during one run, the first shot being fired some three-and-one-half miles away. These seven rounds cleared the deck amidships of all antiaircraft gunner opposition, facilitating additional runs.

"There was much general destruction on her deck. The skip bombing, machine gun strafing, and cannon firing apparently disabled her electrical system because none of her gun turrets were operating. Surely, if operational, her crew would have returned fire. One 75mm projectile penetrated her smoke-

This B-25J of the 486th BS, 340th BG sustained a direct flak hit, which considerably damaged its right wing tip during "Operation Strangle," a mission over southern France; the 486th was based at Corsica. *USAF*

stack and exploded just below deck, blowing a hole in her starboard [right] side. Japanese bodies were seen lying face down just aft of the smokestack. Circles of white foam around her came from near misses by skip bombs, which are effective as direct hits in staving in the ship's steel plates under water.

"One skip bomb made a direct hit on her powder magazine and the vessel exploded amidships. The smaller destroyer was sunk.

"In addition to the two destroyers, the three types of B-25s on this mission sank a small troop transport vessel carrying men and supplies; several troop carrying barges; and, shortly after leaving the scene, the B-25G put a 75mm round into a Japanese transport plane just as it was landing at the southernmost remaining large Japanese-held airfield on New Britain. A quick, second cannon shot wiped out the fleeing survivors from the plane."

**Carl R. Wildner, Lt. Col. USAF (Retired)**
**17th BG, 37th BS**

"As I look back, the Tokyo raid was a marvel of imagination, ingenuity, gung ho, and divine protection. How any such group, inexperienced in war, could have put together such a devastating blow to the Japanese confidence took all of these four factors.

"In February 1942 we flew from Pendleton, Oregon [then the 17th BG's base], to Columbia, South Carolina, and lived in squad tents. I was one of five navigators in the 37th BS with the most experience, and we were asked if we wanted to go on a mission of great importance and secrecy. We looked to each other and said, 'OK.' That's how yours truly volunteered.

"Soon, from a series of short field takeoffs, and one US Navy Lt. Henry L. Miller, later Rear Admiral USN retired, I deduced that we'd be making takeoffs from an aircraft carrier—to bomb Japan!

"One of the marvels of this project is that the auxiliary fuel tanks were designed, built, and installed in about two months. The integral self-sealing wing tanks only held 676 gallons. The auxiliary tanks held another 450 gallons—230 in the one-half bomb bay tank, 160 in the rubber bladder-type tank in the crawl space above the bomb bay (held in by plywood front and back), and sixty in a tank housed within the bottom gun turret area (the turret had been removed). On the Hornet, a decision was made to rope ten five-gallon cans to the back of the bomb bay (it was the job of the radio operator/top turret gunner to knock two holes in each can with the hatchet we carried onboard for emergencies, and pour them into the lower turret tank with a funnel). Thus, on the actual mission, we had a total fuel allotment of 1,176 gallons.

"At the end of March 1942 we flew to McClellan Field near Sacramento, California, to replace pitted propellers. On 1 April we flew to NAS [Naval Air Station] Alameda in Oakland, California. Our plane was left on the dock because it had brake trouble. Sixteen planes were loaded on the Hornet by a Navy crane. All crews were taken aboard. My pilot, Lt. Travis Hoover (later Col. USAF Retired), was assigned to someone else's plane because he was more experienced. The other pilot was very unhappy.

"I had a US Army canvas cot that crowded the room of two USN fighter pilots, next to the anchor chains in the bow of the Hornet.

"The mission: It was supposed to be an evening takeoff, bomb by moonlight, get to China after dawn, and land at Chuchow about fifty miles inland. These Chinese were to put some gas (I understand that a special 130 octane gas was used for the raid) in the wing tanks, then we were to fly to Chungking to turn our planes over to the American

Volunteer Group. It did not work out that way.

"At 7:20 a.m. local time on 18 April 1942 I had just put my B-4 bag and navigator's case in my B-25B (40-2292), when I could see two Japanese fishing boats off the port [left] bow of the Hornet. The Task Force consisted of our two best carriers (the other being the Enterprise), four cruisers, eight destroyers, and two tankers. One cruiser turned and sank the boats with its guns. That blast of orange-colored smoke brought the war closer to me than it had been thus far.

"All navigators went to the ready room for position and course information. Though one of the fishing boats had contacted Japan by radio, the decision was made to proceed with the mission. We were still some 625 miles from Japan instead of 400 miles as desired.

"Lieutenant Colonel Doolittle (later General USAF Retired) took off first and made one circle of the carrier. Hoover took off in half the distance of only about 475ft left of the deck as we had about a 50mph head wind; our plane took off at 70mph.

"We followed Doolittle during the entire trip except over the target. We had nothing to navigate by except the wave tops (we were at 200ft altitude), and we had to guess what the wind was.

"Between dead reckoning [essentially nonobservational navigation by computations of position based on course and distance traveled from a known position], I would transfer gas to one side of the airplane every twenty minutes or so. This meant calling Sgt. Douglas V. Radney [later Maj. USAF Retired] in back to tell him which side to watch the gas cap for an overflow of fuel. Radney and I even rolled up the rubber tank in the crawl space to get every possible drop of fuel out of it. Although we had to transfer fuel to one side or the other every twenty minutes, altogether it took some forty minutes per side because the pumped gas went into the front wing tank, and with a one-way valve, the rear wing tank drained into the front wing tank. That job, transferring the gas on our airplane, was both hectic and dangerous. But at the time, since gas was truly worth its weight in gold, we

weren't much concerned with those factors.

"Two miracles of the mission are first, that sixteen fuel transfer pumps didn't fail and, second, that 448 spark plugs went twelve-to-fourteen hours without a failure.

"We bombed from an altitude of 900ft because Lt. Richard E. Miller, our bombardier, had picked the wrong target—perhaps fortunately, because Doolittle's gunner reported that debris from our bombs went higher than our plane, but luckily, behind our plane.

"Hoover [our pilot] and I had an argument of about twenty minutes duration. He wanted to get out of there [Japanese airspace], and I wanted to save gas as we were burning a little more than we were supposed to. Besides I said, there were no fighters after us and we weren't being pursued by flak. Finally over Tokyo Bay I got him to pull the props and mixture back. One reason we got 1mph rather than 2mph, was that after takeoff, we set the props at 1,475rpm [revolutions per minute]. As the load lightened, and after our discussion, we pulled them back to 1,360rpm. At this prop speed we could talk in a normal tone of voice within the cabin.

"We were forced to belly land [landing gear retracted] in a rice paddy near the coast of China because we did not have the gas to climb over the hills to get inland. We probably had fifty gallons of gas left crossing the coast, and a mere twenty gallons when we bellied in.

"With all of the things that went wrong, it is amazing that there were not more deaths and injuries. Many of the airplanes flew alone and never saw the coast of China because they had climbed into clouds and rain and darkness. Their crews did not know where they were because they had no navigation aids (land features, etc.). They were forced to bail out into who knew what when one of their plane's engines quit.

"It took one hour to launch all sixteen airplanes off the carrier. After some twelve to fourteen hours of mission time, one plane landed in Russia, three planes crash landed in the waters off the coast of China, and the other twelve planes—some manned, some unmanned, crash landed in China."

*Chapter 6*

# Foreign Users

Following the sneak attack on Pearl Harbor, Hawaii, on 7 December 1941 the United States and the United Kingdom declared war on Japan. In turn, Germany and Italy declared war on the United States—and on 11 December 1941, the US Congress declared war on those two countries. Suddenly America, its Allies, and its friends had entered into the all-out global battle to be called World War II.

Sometime before the United States had declared war on Germany, Italy, Japan, and their cohorts, however, a number of US allies and friends were already at war in Europe and elsewhere. And to fight a war successfully, America's allies and friends needed new and improved airplanes. The North American B-25 was one such airplane, and by the time the United States entered the war, plans were already being made for US allies and friends to get them. In fact, on 30 June 1941, some five months before the attack on Pearl Harbor, the Netherlands had signed a contract with North American to procure 162 B-25C-5-NA airplanes for its Netherlands East Indies Air Force (NEIAF). And on 14 January 1942, Britain and China were scheduled to receive 150 B-25C-10-NAs

B-25J (44-31162) destined for duty in the Russian Air Force. Under lend-lease, Russia received 870 Mitchells—B-25B/C/D/H/J models. *Rockwell*

(Britain) and 150 B-25C-15-NAs (China). Britain's Royal Air Force (RAF) had already received twenty-three B-25B airplanes, which it dubbed the Mitchell I.

During the war, out of the sixteen countries that made up the Allied Forces (Australia, Brazil, Belgium, Great Britain, Canada, China, Denmark, France, Greece, New Zealand, the Netherlands, Norway, Poland, Russia, South Africa, and Yugoslavia), nine countries—Australia, Brazil, China, Canada, France, Great Britain, the Netherlands, Poland, and Russia—employed the B-25 in their air forces.

## Australia

Squadrons 2 and 18 of the Royal Australian Air Force (RAAF) received thirty-nine and eleven B-25 Mitchells, respectively, for a relatively small total of fifty aircraft. These Mitchells were B-25C, B-25D, B-25G, B-25H, and B-25J models; RAAF serial numbers A47-1 through A47-50. For the most part these B-25s fought in the Netherlands East Indies (now Republic of Indonesia) in the Southwest Pacific with a number of the Royal Netherlands Air Force (RNAF).

## Brazil

The *Forca Aerea Brazileira*, under lend-lease during World War II, received twenty-nine Mitchells. The first of these being six B-25Bs. It also got one B-25C and twenty-one B-25Js. After the war, from July 1946 to October 1947, Brazil

obtained another sixty-four B-25 airplanes; mostly, B-25Js.

## China

The Chinese Nationalist Air Force (CNAF) and the Chinese Air Force (CAF) received B-25C, B-25D, B-25H, and B-25J airplanes. It is not documented how many of each model were received. It is known, however, that more than 100 B-25C and B-25D aircraft were received by the CNAF. And it got at least twenty-eight B-25Hs and six B-25Js. Most or all of these B-25s served in the China-Burma (now Myanma)-India (CBI) Theater of Operations. The People's Republic of China obtained an unknown quantity of B-25 airplanes that had been forsaken when the CNAF and other Nationalist Chinese forces were forced to escape to Formosa (Taiwan).

## Canada

The Royal Canadian Air Force (RCAF) received via Great Britain 173 B-25s; RCAF serial numbers 5200 through 5283, FW 220 through FW 280, 891 through 894, HD 310 through HD 345, KL 133 through KL-161, KJ 641 and KJ 764, and FK 164/166/171/176/177/178/180; B-25Bs, B-25Ds, and B-25Js. Six of these, all with unknown serial numbers, were B-25Js. In addition to protecting its own coastlines, Canada's RCAF Mitchells served in the ETO. Although it is not documented, some RCAF B-25s might have fought in the MTO. Like the

A B-25D (Mitchell II) of the RAF unloads its bombs on a German target in Europe. *Rockwell*

British B-25s, these were called Mitchell Is, IIs, and IIIs.

## France

The *Armee de l'Air*, with one squadron—342 Squadron, which served within the British RAF—employed about thirty B-25C and B-25D (Mitchell II) aircraft. These were deployed in the ETO, and possibly, in the MTO.

## Great Britain

The RAF operated a large number of Mitchell I (B-25B), Mitchell II (B-25C/D), and Mitchell III (B-25J) airplanes. Used in the European, Mediterranean,

A pristine B-25J (44-31387) that belonged to the Republic of China. Turrets and blister guns have been removed, meaning it was modified to serve as a transport plane. *Campbell Archives*

Dutch Air Force B-25Cs on their way to German targets in France. *Rockwell*

and CBI theaters of operations—and in the Northern, Central, and Southern Atlantic Ocean areas, RAF Mitchells were used by the known units as follows:

Aeroplane and Armament Experimental Establishment, Boscomb Down, England; Bombing Trials Unit; Royal Aircraft Establishment, Farnborough, England; 2 Group Support Unit; 13 Operational Training Unit; 98 Squadron; 21 Squadron; 45 Group (RCAF); 111 Operational Training Unit; 114 Squadron; 180 Squadron; 226 Squadron; 305 Squadron (Polish Air Force); 313 Ferry Training Unit; 320 Squadron (Royal Netherlands Naval Air Service); 342 Squadron (French Air Force); and 1482 Bomber Gunnery Unit. Great Britain, in all, received at least 870 B-25 airplanes; twenty-three B-25Bs (Mitchell I), 533 B-25C/Ds (Mitchell II), and 314 B-25Js (Mitchell III). These were shared with two United Kingdom (British Commonwealth) nations—Australia and Canada.

An RAF crew with their Mitchell II (B-25D) named *Daily Delivery*. That's how the Brits dressed. *Rockwell*

A RCAF B-25J (44-30652) that was restored to make the air show circuits. It belonged to RCAF 418 Squadron and is named "City of Edmonton." *Author's Collection*

A beautifully restored B-25J (Mitchell III) at an unknown British outdoor museum. *Campbell Archives*

## Netherlands

The Royal Netherlands Air Force (RNethAF), the Royal Netherlands Naval Aviation Service (RNethNAS), and the Royal Netherlands Flying School (RNethFS), through the Netherlands Purchasing Commission (NPC) during World War II, procured a large number of B-25 Mitchells. The planes were used in a number of theaters of operations, including the Netherlands East Indies (NEI) in the Southwest Pacific, the Northeast Atlantic, CBI, and Europe.

For the required training of its B-25 Mitchell pilots, the RNethFS in 1941 and 1942, which was based in the United States at Jackson, Mississippi, operated at least fifteen B-25Cs and five B-25Ds. The survivors were returned to the USAAF in early 1944, and apparently, these B-25s never did see actual combat.

Through a loan agreement with Great Britain, 320 Squadron of the RAF released some sixty-seven of its B-25C and B-25D (Mitchell II) airplanes to the RNethNAS. Survivors were returned to the RAF.

And through lend-lease and other allocations, the RNethAF received at least another 157 B-25C, B-25D, and B-25J airplanes for use primarily in the Netherlands East Indies and the CBI Theater of Operations.

## Poland

The 305 Squadron of the Polish Air Force operated at least twelve B-25s. Like those of France, they served within the British RAF. These were deployed in the ETO.

## Russia

The Russian Air Force received through lend-lease 870 B-25B, B-25C, B-25D, B-25H, and B-25J airplanes. The amount of each model is unknown; the serial numbers are also unknown.

## Postwar Users

After the war, the North American B-25 Mitchell was purchased by another ten foreign countries—Argentina, Bolivia, Chile, Columbia, Cuba, the Dominican Republic, Mexico, Peru, Uruguay, and Venezuela.

## Argentina

Under civilian registrations, through US government surplus sales, Argentina purchased three B-25J airplanes for use in the private sector. It is not known if any of these were used by Argentina's Air Force, the *Fuerza Aerea Argentina*.

## Bolivia

The *Fuerza Aerea Boliviana* reportedly, though not confirmed, might have procured six B-25J airplanes in 1947 and 1948.

## Chile

The *Fuerza Aerea de Chile* received a dozen B-25Js in October 1947.

## Columbia

The *Fuerza Aerea Columbiana* procured a trio of B-25J airplanes in July 1947.

## Cuba

The *Fuerza Aerea Ejercito de Cuba* is known to have obtained as many as six B-25 airplanes (models and serial numbers, however, are unknown).

## Dominican Republic

The *Cuerpo de Aviocion Dominicana* got one B-25 in 1951. It is believed that this airplane was converted to serve as a very important persons (VIP) transport.

## Mexico

The *Fuerza Aerea Mexicana* received three B-25J airplanes in late 1945.

## Peru

The *Fuerza Aerea del Peru (Grupo 21)* procured eight B-25Js in July 1947. In 1964, six of these had been reassigned to the 21 Bomb Squadron, Chiclayo, Peru.

## Uruguay

The *Fuerza Aerea Uruguaya* procured an undocumented number of B-25s; however, it is known that it got at least twenty-two B-25J airplanes beginning in 1950.

## Venezuela

The *Fuerza Aereas Venezolanas* might have received as many as forty B-25J airplanes. In 1957 Venezuela contracted the L. B. Smith Aircraft Corporation, Miami, Florida, to completely overhaul nine of these B-25Js. Their final disposition is unknown.

A B-25J Mitchell III of the RAAF (unknown squadron) flies near Brisbane, Australia, circa 1944. The RAAF played a major role in the Southwest Pacific Theater of Operations throughout World War II. *RAAF via Ernest R. McDowell*

Three Russian Air Force airmen talk with pilot USAAF Lt. Bill Dotson (at right), after one of a number of tour flights throughout the MTO, circa 1944. Senior pilot Lieutenant Roschenko (next to Dotson) served as copilot during the tour of USAAF air bases. *USAF*

Excellent study of an RAAF B-25J on a flight over down under. The airplane was employed by 18 Squadron from April 1945 to May 1950 when it was sold to a private owner. It was never used in combat. *Ernest R. McDowell Collection*

*Chapter 7*

# Mitchells in the Navy: The PBJs

**R**ivalries between the branches of the US armed forces exist—especially when it comes to the procurement of a certain type of airplane. So when one service buys another service's plane for its own use it simply means that a plane fits its requirement as well. This rarely happens. So in late 1941, when the US Navy started to look for another land-based patrol bomber, it settled on the North American B-25 Mitchell.

As its purchasing agent, the US Navy initiated a procurement program to outfit the US Marine Corps with what became the PBJ (P-Patrol, B-Bomber, J-North American) series of aircraft. In all, for dedicated antisubmarine warfare, the US Navy bought B-25 Mitchells in six versions—the PBJ-1, PBJ-1C, PBJ-1D, PBJ-1G, PBJ-1H, and the PBJ-1J. Thus, the PBJ-1 was the US Marine Corps (USMC) version of the Inglewood-built B-25B; the PBJ-1C was the USMC version of the Inglewood-built B-25C; the PBJ-1D was the USMC version of the Kansas City-built B-25D; the one-of-a-kind PBJ-1G was the USMC version of the Inglewood-built B-25G; the PBJ-1H was the USMC version of the Inglwood-built B-25H; and the PBJ-1J was the USMC version of the Kansas City- built

A flock of new B-25Ds grace the flight line at NAA's Kansas City plant with "Old Glory" waving good-bye to the one being towed away for a flight. *Rockwell*

A PBJ-1D flies high over clouds on a check flight prior to delivery. *Rockwell*

A Kansas City paint shop employee puts the finishing touches on the new USN insignia, circa June 1942. The PBJ-1D, shown here, was the first PBJ model to be built at NAA's Kansas City plant. *Rockwell*

"It's a Navy ship, all right!" Toolboxes in hands, assembly workers prepare to go to work on this PBJ-1D, circa June 1943, when heavy rains caused flooding. *Rockwell*

B-25J. Purchased by the US Navy and used by the US Marine Corps, the PBJ, like the B-25, was well received.

## The PBJ-1

It remains undocumented as to exactly how many PBJ-1s were procured from the relatively small procurement batch of 119 B-25B airplanes. It is known, however, that the first PBJ-1 squadron—VMB-413—was established at Cherry Point, North Carolina, on 1 March 1943. The airplane was extensively evaluated at Patuxent River, Maryland, where US Navy types are tested. For the immediate training of PBJ pilots and copilots (USMC aviators were single-engine pilots at the time), navigators, gunners, and so on, VMB-413 squadron became the PBJ training and transition squadron. Those who first

trained with VMB-413 formed the core for following USMC PBJ squadrons.

There were sixteen USMC PBJ squadrons in all and each one was established at Cherry Point, North Carolina. These included: VMB-413; VMB-423, VMB-433, and VMB-443 established on 15 September 1943; VMB-611, VMB-612, and VMB-613 established on 10 October 1943; VMB-614, VMB-621, VMB-622, VMB-623, VMB-624, VMB-453, VMB-463, VMB-473, and VMB-483 followed (the establishment dates of these last nine PBJ squadrons are not known by the author).

The PBJ-1 was similar to its B-25B counterpart with the exception of being equipped to lay mines, deploy depth charges, and launch torpedoes. Used primarily for coastal defense, their mission was to pursue and destroy German

The PBJ-1H, like its B-25H counterpart, featured improved armor and armament. Its four nose guns, four side guns, two top turret guns, two waist guns, two tail turret guns, and 75mm cannon made this PBJ much more deadlier than its earlier -1, -1C, 1-D, and -1G counterparts. *Rockwell*

and Japanese submarines in the Atlantic and Pacific oceans; they also served as strafers against surface shipping.

## The PBJ-1C and PBJ-1D

The USMC received fifty PBJ-1Cs from NAA's Inglewood plant and 151 PBJ-1Ds from NAA's Kansas City plant. And like the B-25C was basically a B-25D (their main difference being that they had not been manufactured at the

A factory-fresh PBJ-1H banks right to return to Inglewood during a check flight over the Pacific. *Rockwell*

An excellent color study of a PBJ-1H. On 15 November 1944, one PBJ-1H (BuNo 35277) accomplished aircraft carrier trials on the USS *Shangri La*. Although those carrier take-off and landing trials were successful, PBJs never did operate from carriers. *Rockwell*

same location), the PBJ-1C was fundamentally a PBJ-1D.

For the hunting and killing of enemy shipping—both on the surface and under the oceans and seas, the PBJ-1Cs and PBJ-1Ds were equipped with the following armament:

• The AN/APS-3 search radar and a Loran (long-range navigation) system.

• Blister-type machine gun packs on either side of the forward fuselage housing two .50cal machine guns each.

• Up to three nose-mounted .50cal machine guns in varied configurations; fixed or flexible mounts.

• Modified bomb bay to carry mines, depth charges, or one high-explosive torpedo.

• Ten underwing attachment points (five under each wing) to carry unguided 5in diameter high-velocity aircraft rockets (HVAR) with high-explosive warheads.

## The PBJ-1G

For unknown reasons, the USN procured only one PBJ-1G, and unfortunately, there is no documentation of this one-of-a-kind Naval Mitchell.

## The PBJ-1H

The USMC held the PBJ-1H in high esteem, and in July 1944, the USN accomplished a number of carrier launches and trappings on board the USS *Shangri La* off Cape May, Virginia. And in a letter to NAA the USN reported, in part, the following:

Arrested landing tests with a 26,250-pound gross weight were accomplished during a two-day exercise. Seventeen landings were made, some of them from ten to fifteen feet off center and into as little as six mile per hour wind in some instances.

Lt. Cmdr. H. S. Bottomley, the officer-commanding, in charge of all these tests, said, "the results of the tests so far have been very favorable." He recommended, however, that the length of the hock [arresting hook] be increased due to the fact that when the airplane is landed with the nose down [three-point or horizontal attitude], after a late cut [power] signal from the signal officer, the nose wheel strut tends to collapse and the main gear oleos tend to extend carrying the hock completely over the cables. The necessary rework is being accomplished by removing the tail-skid [bumper] and splicing an additional ten inches into the arresting hook shaft just forward of the hook shank. It has been decided that the

ideal landing attitude is from three to five degrees, tail heavy, however it is not always possible for a pilot to land the airplane in exactly these attitudes, especially on a carrier deck.

Bottomley also recommended that the hook installation and the airplane structure be beefed up to withstand a horizontal deceleration of 2 Gs; the present structure and hook installation will take 1.5 Gs with a safety margin of only one percent at some points according to the stress analysis submitted by the NAA Engineering Department.

In the end, however, the USN never did adapt any version of the PBJ series to carrier-based duties. Ironically, after the war, NAA provided the USN with its first large carrier-based airplane—the AJ Savage series.

A PBJ-1H equipped with the AN/APS-3 search radar system and four underwing (two on each wing) 5in rockets. *Rockwell*

## The PBJ-1J

The PBJ-1J was the ultimate version of the PBJ series. And like its B-25J counterpart, it was the most heavilyarmed version with up to eighteen .50cal machine guns.

In addition to antishipping maneuvers, the PBJ-1J airplane had been optimized to attack and destroy ground-based targets with both unguided and guided rockets. And as a dedicated strafer, it was just as deadly as the US-AAF B-25G/H/J aircraft. To the USN, but more important to the USMC units that operated them (see below), the PBJs were everything that the B-25s were to the USAAF. Simply stated, it did not matter what mission the PBJ was called upon to do, it just went out and did it. Thus the PBJ, like its B-25 counterpart, was a Mitchell in the first degree. And together they helped win World War II.

Excellent in-flight color view of a new Kansas City-built PBJ-1J, circa 1944. The USN PBJ-1J, like its USAAF B-25J cousin, was the definitive version of the Mitchell bomber. *Rockwell*

## USMC Combat Squadrons

| User Squadron | Base of Operations (as of early 1945) |
|---|---|
| VMB-412 | Endenton, North Carolina |
| VMB-413 | Endenton, North Carolina |
| VMB-423 | Pacific Theater |
| VMB-433 | Pacific Theater |
| VMB-443 | Pacific Theater |
| VMB-453 | Cherry Point, North Carolina |
| VMB-463 | Cherry Point, North Carolina |
| VMB-473 | Cherry Point, North Carolina |
| VMB-483 | Kingston, North Carolina |
| VMB-611 | Cherry Point, North Carolina |
| VMB-612 | Pacific Theater |
| VMB-613 | Pacific Theater |
| VMB-614 | Newport, Arizona |
| VMB-621 | Cherry Point, North Carolina |
| VMB-622 | Newport, Arizona |
| VMB-623 | Cherry Point, North Carolina |
| VMB-624 | Cherry Point, North Carolina |

Piloted by USN Lt. Cdr. Bottomley, this PBJ-1H lands on the USS *Shangri La* during aircraft carrier qualification trials late in 1944. The plane has just caught one of the arresting cables. *D. W. Lucabaugh Collection via Ernest R. McDowell*

KEEP
OUT

Previous page
B-25Js in final assembly at Kansas City, circa mid-1944. *Rockwell*

As can be seen from the list above, the USMC VMB (V—heavier than air, M—USMC squadron, B—bombardment) squadrons were employed in the United States to defend the coasts, and in the Pacific Theater of Operations to attack and destroy enemy land and sea targets.

All in all, during the fiscal years of 1943 through 1945, the USN procured 706 Mitchell bomber airplanes for use by the USMC; that is, 188 in 1943, 395 in 1944, and 123 in 1945 (see appendix B for the PBJ acquisition summary).

A PBJ-1J, identical to the B-25J but in naval dress, shows off its complement of armament and a radar radome on its right-hand wing tip.

PBJs carried nose-mounted, wing-mounted, and belly-mounted radomes. *D. W. Lucabaugh Collection via Ernest R. McDowell*

Extremely rare photograph of a postwar US Coast Guard B-25J (44-31357) at an unknown location. This is proof that all branches of the

US Armed Forces used Mitchell bombers. *D. W. Lucabaugh Collection via Ernest R. McDowell*

A restored, privately owned PBJ-1J shows off its *Pacific Princess* nose art. *Campbell Archives*

*Chapter 8*

# VIP Transports, Advanced Trainers, Radar and Fire Control System Trainers

The basic B-25 airframe could be configured for other purposes. As proved, it did not matter whether it was the original straight-winged B-25 or the gull-winged B-25J. From the eight primary Mitchell variants—the B-25, B-25A, B-25B, B-25C, B-25D, B-25G, B-25H, and B-25J—a number of VIP or very important person(s) transports, advanced trainers, and radar/fire control system trainers emerged. Additionally, in the postwar years, other obscure derivatives of the prolific B-25 came about.

## The VIP Transports

Beginning in late 1942, North American redesigned and modified five different B-25 airplanes to serve as VIP transport aircraft. Prior to June 1948, when the prefix "R" was changed to mean Reconnaissance, these VIP transports were designated as RB-25s (at the time "R" meant Restricted, not to be used on combat missions). After June 1948, surviving RB-25s were redesignated VB-25s—the prefix "V" meaning Staff or very important person(s). For clarity, however, these five aircraft will be referred to by the original designations, as the RB-25 (one example), the RB-25C (one example), and the RB-25J (three examples).

Interior view of N5126N (the *Executive Transport* plane's civil registration number) shows its plush aft seating area. *Rockwell*

## The RB-25 (40-2165)

NAA had three aircraft assembly plants in operation during World War II (Inglewood, California; Kansas City, Kansas; and Dallas, Texas). Company executives and other key personnel, such as engineers and technical representatives, required an efficient mode of travel to those three factories and to other places throughout the country. Moreover, they would often have to depart at a moment's notice. Therefore, regularly scheduled commercial airlines, which in many cases did not operate close enough to many of the locations needed to be visited by NAA personnel, were useless for the most part. To visit their factories, subcontractors, and military establishments around the nation, NAA decided to create a Personnel Transport. After careful analyses of all available types of aircraft, NAA decided that one of its own products was best—the B-25.

It was November 1942 and wartime demands did not allow for the modification of a new B-25. So, with 280 flight test hours already in its logbook, and because many of its assemblies were not applicable to other production aircraft (it had been built mostly by hand on temporary jigs), the first B-25 airplane was bailed back to NAA for modification into the first of five Personnel Transport aircraft.

To create the first RB-25, dubbed *Whiskey Express*, tactical equipment—

bomb racks, machine gun mounts, and so on—were stripped out of the fuselage. Windows on either side of the fuselage were installed; two passenger seats were installed just behind the pilot and copilot seats forward of the bomb bay; five more passenger seats were placed behind the bomb bay; a bed was fitted above the bomb bay; the bomb bay was transformed into a baggage area; a desk and intercom system were installed in the aft fuselage for business matters during flights from one place to another;

A postwar RB-25 (formerly F-10) arrives at Kansas City to undergo modification for civilian use. *Rockwell*

NAA's first transport, nicknamed the *Whiskey Express* being towed from its parking area at Inglewood. The airplane was damaged beyond repair during a crash landing on 8 January 1945. *Rockwell*

and, to house navigation and radio gear, the framed glass nose was replaced with a solid nose. Its unbroken dihedral wing had been replaced earlier with the broken dihedral wing.

This first RB-25 airplane served NAA's personnel and friends well until early January 1945, when it was sched

Gen. Henry H. "Hap" Arnold. During forty-one years of active service in the US Army and Air Force, he compiled a record unparalleled in military history. Universally acknowledged as the father of the modern US Air Force, he took charge of the then US Army Air Corps in 1938 when it was a relatively tiny collection of twenty thousand men and a few hundred planes. By 1944, under the whip of his compelling, relentless, and often unreasonable dynamism, it grew into an organization of 2.4 million men and women and more than eighty thousand aircraft. Never before or since has a military machine of such size and technical complexity been created in so short a period. At the height of World War II, General Arnold commanded the largest, mightiest Air Force the world had ever seen and perhaps will ever see again. People who knew "Hap" Arnold weren't surprised that he died virtually broke. Money had never attracted him. Airplanes were his obsession. The Wright brothers had taught him to fly in 1911, and he was the holder of US Army Pilot's License Number Two. He spent more than half his life fighting for the development of air power and air transportation. *Rockwell*

uled for various maintenance checks, including the change of its engines. Work was completed on 8 January 1945 and it was scheduled for a check flight.

Piloted by Ed Stewart (NAA pilot assigned to the *Whiskey Express)* and copiloted by Theron Morgan, the airplane's routine check flight out of Mines Field ensued; crew chief Jack Maholm checked off items on the check list. Two checks, one at a time, were to feather each engine. One engine was feathered, but it refused to unfeather. The premier B-25's demise came next.

During final approach to Mines Field, with only one engine providing power, the plane's landing gear refused to lock after it had been extended. After touchdown, and during its emergency landing and roll-out to a stop, the unlocked landing gear collapsed and the plane crashed. A crash was expected, so Stewart used an area of the airfield that would not damage the runway. There were no injuries to the three crewmen nor any fire that might have occurred on a spark-producing paved runway. After the crash, it was determined that the landing gear's refusal to down-lock was the result of inadequate hydraulic locking pressure. Since the airplane did not have enough power to reach climb-out

General Arnold's second B-25 transport as it appeared after the war, now designated VB-25N. Arnold had used this plane until January 1946, and for a time, it carried the designation VB-25J. *David W. Menard Collection*

A modified postwar RB-25. Unfortunately, during its first flight after modification, its landing gear failed on landing and it bellied in (note bent props). *Rockwell*

NAA's *Executive Transport*, the second B-25 type to be converted for company use, was formerly a USN PBJ-1J (BuNo 35848). *Rockwell*

Interior of NAA's *Executive Transport* details its modernized interior. The photographer is located where the bomb bay used to be. *Rockwell*

speed and build locking pressure during a go-around, it was forced to land when it did. This historic airplane, the forerunner to 9,888 additional B-25s, suffered extensive airframe structure damage and could not be rebuilt. What ultimately became of it remains unclear.

### The RB-25C (41-13251)

One B-25C-1-NA, after a series of modifications, became the second of five Personnel Transport aircraft to be produced. As it happened, USAAF commanding General Henry H. "Hap" Arnold visited NAA in early 1943. He needed a personnel transport for himself and his staff while jaunting all over the nation. Impressed with NAA's RB-25, he soon arranged for a B-25C to be bailed back to its builder so it could be converted into his transport. Using government funds, North American's Field Service Department was authorized to proceed. And in June 1943, the conversion was complete. On 19 June 1943, NAA's Robert C. "Bob" Chilton, made the first flight on General Arnold's RB-25C. After additional company test hops and one four-hour USAAF check flight on 10 July 1943, the airplane was

A MATS (Military Air Transport Service) CB-25J (44-30457) hauling cargo. Black engine nacelles are noteworthy. *USAF via Tony Landis*

delivered to General Arnold. USAAF Col. Claire Peterson was Arnold's pilot.

In the summer of 1945, with more than 300 flying hours in its logbook, the RB-25C became a war asset and it was placed in storage for its final disposition—more than likely headed for the postwar aircraft boneyard to be scrapped. In 1947, however, it was sold to a civilian as a plush business plane. Then in November 1948, it was sold to Bankers Life and Casualty Company in Chicago, Illinois, with whom it remained until June 1951, when it was bought for a tidy sum by one Howard Hughes. Hughes retained it until 1962, and today, after a number of other owners, it is reportedly still airworthy.

## The RB-25J (43-4030)

In February 1944, at the request of Gen. Dwight D. "Ike" Eisenhower, then Supreme Allied Commander for the upcoming invasion of Europe, NAA received government monies to convert another B-25 into a Personnel Transport for Ike and his staff. Beginning in March 1944, at its Inglewood plant, NAA took an early production B-25J-1-NC airplane and quickly converted it into Ike's plane. The reason for the urgency, we know now, was D-Day in Europe on 6 June 1944. It is known that Ike was moving all over England and elsewhere in his RB-25J before D-Day. Ike's plane was created, flight tested, and delivered overseas to him only three (or less) months after NAA had received the official go-ahead.

The first RB-25J returned to the United States after VE-Day and, in 1947, it entered into cargo-carrying duties at Bolling AAF, Washington, D.C.; it had been redesignated CB-25J. In 1948, redesignated VB-25J, it began service with the 1100th Special Air Mission Group and transported VIPs throughout the nation. In December 1958, it was flown to Davis-Monthan AFB in Arizona to await scrapping at what is known today as the Air Force's Aerospace Maintenance and Regeneration Center; it was stricken from USAF inventory in February 1959. Luckily, the historically valuable airplane was sold to a civilian as government surplus. And in 1981, after several owners, this historic airplane was procured by the USAF for permanent display at Ellsworth AFB in South Dakota. In time it was restored fully as

Ike's plane, and today it resides in that air base's museum.

General Arnold liked Ike's RB-25J airplane somewhat more than his own. And with little or no trouble, he was able to trade in his airplane on a new one. Again with government funds, a later model B-25J-15-NC was set aside for North American to create the number four Personnel Transport—Arnold's second. Produced exactly like Ike's, and piloted by NAA's Ed Virgin, it made its first flight at Mines Field on 24 November 1944. It was found to be sound and was delivered to Arnold in December 1944. He used it until January 1946. As a VB-25J it stayed in USAF service until 1953 at which time it was removed from USAF inventory. Three civilian owners operated it until 1972. It disappeared from US civil registry and its final disposition remains unclear.

After NAA's RB-25 crashed on 8 January 1945, and after it had been deter-

mined that plane would not be rebuilt, North American management opted to create its second Personnel Transport. A B-25J was converted for that purpose in mid-1945. Built to nearly identical specifications as Ike's and Hap's RB-25Js, and flown by Ed Stewart (pilot) and George Krebs (copilot), it made its first flight as an RB-25J on 18 October 1945.

Then on 27 February 1946, after only some thirty hours of flying time, the airplane and its crew were lost during a check flight over the Pacific Ocean near Malibu, California. During the ill-fated flight, NAA pilot Joe Barton radioed that the plane was burning. An explosion came next and the plane crashed at sea. Barton and two other crewmen died that tragic day.

## The Advanced Trainers

The USAAF converted sixty B-25Cs, B-25Ds, B-25Gs, and B-25Hs (no detailed breakdown by variants has been

A B-25J that was used as a target tow airplane, Vance AFB in Oklahoma. *Campbell Archives*

A solid nose TB-25J (44-28847) the Strategic Air Command (SAC) used in the 1950s. Note SAC crest on nose. *David W. Menard Collection*

A CB-25J used by MATS in the 1950s. *USAF via Tony Landis*

documented) into Advanced Training (AT) aircraft. Respectively, these were redesignated AT-24A, AT-24B, AT-24C, and AT-24D. In the late 1940s, however, survivors were respectively redesignated TB-25D, TB-25G, TB-25C, and TB-25J. During the war, as well as after the war, these were used as multiengine training and transition aircraft for USAF pilots assigned to multiengine propeller-driven aircraft.

### The "Executive Transport"

In 1949, in hope of generating peacetime business, North American procured a low-time PBJ-1J (BuNo 35848) from US government surplus to convert into what it would call the "Executive Transport." Its conversion was complete in early 1950.

To convert the plane, NAA designed and installed a longer and wider nose section forward of the wings. This longer and wider nose, complete with a Convair 240 airliner windshield and in-

strument panel and six forward-facing seats, was somewhat bulbous. This led some people to call NAA's "Executive Transport" the "Bulbous-Nosed B-25." In any event, it was ready to fly.

On 15 February 1950, with Ed Virgin at the controls, this unique transport made a successful flight at Mines Field. It could attain 300mph at 28,000ft.

To find possible VIP transport customers, the "Executive Transport" began a nationwide tour of USAF air bases starting in California with Mather and Hamilton. On 25 March 1950, to return to California, it departed Wright Field. The return to Inglewood was going fine until the airplane was just east of Phoenix, Arizona. It suddenly flew into heavy turbulence as it entered a storm front. The airplane could not handle the severe turbulence, and after structural failure, it crashed to destruction, killing all seven on board. It was piloted by Miles Towner and copiloted by Jack Steppe, both of NAA customer relations.

No orders were forthcoming and NAA's proposed "Executive Transport" program was terminated.

### Pilot, Radar, and Fire Control System Trainers

The USAF wanted to convert a number of surplus Mitchell B-25s for pilot, radar, and fire control system training. To do this, the USAF took bids from NAA, Hayes Aircraft, and Hughes Aircraft. North American was eliminated. Hayes of Birmingham, Alabama, and Hughes of Culver City, California, prevailed. The former would create the pilot trainers, and the latter the radar and fire control system trainers.

Hayes stripped more than 600 B-25Js and completed them as TB-25J-NC pilot trainer airplanes; Hughes modified 117 with its own E-1 radar and fire control system for TB-25K-NC radar trainer airplanes; Hayes stripped ninety and finished them as TB-25L-NC pilot trainer airplanes; Hughes modified forty with its own E-5 radar and fire control system for TB-25M-NC radar trainer airplanes; and Hayes stripped forty-seven B-25s and completed them as TB-25N-NC pilot trainer aircraft with uprated R-2600-29A engines. These conversion programs ended in 1955 with all aircraft delivered to the USAF.

# Conclusion

On 6 August 1940, the premier B-25, a "paper airplane" less than a year earlier, made its debut as a real airplane. It made its maiden flight thirteen days later. On 19 August 1990, the B-25 Mitchell turned fifty. To celebrate the occasion, dozens of surviving B-25s took to the skies throughout the year. Designed to commemorate this unique airplane and how it helped to preserve freedom around the globe in World War II, the B-25's fiftieth anniversary observance was well received.

On 18 April 1942—twenty months after the B-25's premier flight—sixteen B-25Bs launched from the USS *Hornet* and to carry Lt. Col. Jimmy Doolittle and his seventy-nine Tokyo raiders to strike back at Japan for Pearl Harbor. On 18 April 1992, the fiftieth anniversary of that historic event came to pass. In fact, two privately owned B-25s, "Heavenly Body" and "In The Mood," launched from the *Ranger* to reenact the Doolittle Raid. After the Doolittle Raid in 1942, the B-25 helped turn the tide in favor of the United States, its Allies, and its friends.

Surprisingly, when one considers the plight of other World War II aircraft (most were destroyed in combat or in scrap yards), many privately owned B-25s are still flying all around the world. Truly the B-25, with its excellent handling, performance, and adaptability, proved to be one of the most potent combat aircraft in World War II. Success in every combat theater earned it the right of being named after Billy Mitchell—America's best-known champion of bombardment with aircraft and advocate of air power.

Interestingly, in a ceremony at Eglin AFB, Florida, on 21 May 1960, the last B-25 Mitchell was retired from active USAF service. That retirement ceremony marked nineteen years of duty.

The B-25 Mitchell and its many thousands of combat crew members live on in this warbird history.

*Appendix A*

# B-25 Production Summary

| Designation | Amount | Serial Number(s) | Notes of Interest |
|---|---|---|---|
| B-25 | 24 | 40-2165/-2188 | First nine examples were originally built with unbroken dihedral wings; one (40-2165) modified to RB-25 |
| RB-25 | 1 | 40-2165 | Formerly B-25 number one (see above); used by NAA personnel |
| B-25A | 40 | 40-2189/-2228 | |
| B-25B | 14 | 40-2229/-2242 | |
| B-25B | 1 | 40-2243 | Crashed prior to USAAF acceptance; not counted in production total |
| B-25B | 105 | 40-2244/-2348 | 23 to Great Britain |
| B-25C | 605 | 41-12434/-13038 | |
| B-25C-1-NA | 258 | 41-13039/-13296 | One (41-13251) modified to RB-25C; another (41-13296) modified to B-25G prototype |
| RB-25C | 1 | 41-13251 | Formerly a B-25C-1-NA (see above); used by Gen. Arnold and staff officers |
| B-25C-5-NA | 162 | 42-53332/-53493 | To the Netherlands |
| B-25C-10-NA | 150 | 42-32233/-32382 | To Great Britain; one (42-32281) to XB-25E; another (unknown serial) to XB-25F; another (42-32372) modified to B-25H prototype, named "Mortimer II" |
| B-25C-15-NA | 150 | 42-32383/-32532 | To China |
| B-25C-20-NA | 200 | 42-64502/-64701 | |
| B-25C-25-NA | 100 | 42-64702/-64801 | |
| B-25D | 200 | 41-29648/-29847 | |
| B-25D-1-NC | 100 | 41-29848/-29947 | |
| B-25D-5-NC | 225 | 41-29948/-30172 | |
| B-25D-10-NA | 180 | 41-30173/-30352 | |
| B-25D-15-NC | 18 | 41-30353/-30532 | |
| B-25D-15-NC | 315 | 41-30533/-30847 | |
| B-25D-20-NC | 25 | 42-87113/-87137 | |
| B-25D-25-NC | 315 | 42-87138/-87452 | |
| B-25D-30-NC | 160 | 42-87453/-87612 | |
| B-25D-30-NC | 340 | 43-3280/-3619 | |
| B-25D-35-NC | 250 | 43-3620/-3869 | |
| F-10 | 7 | 41-29875/-29881 | One (41-29877) to Canada |
| F-10 | 6 | 41-29883/-29888 | One (41-29886) to Canada |
| F-10 | 1 | 41-29924 | To Canada |
| F-10 | 2 | 41-29926/-29927 | |
| F-10 | 2 | 41-29929/-29930 | |
| F-10 | 1 | 41-29932 | |
| F-10 | 1 | 41-29970 | |
| F-10 | 1 | 41-29984 | |
| F-10 | 5 | 41-29987/-29991 | |
| F-10 | 1 | 41-30132 | |
| F-10 | 1 | 41-30181 | |
| F-10 | 1 | 41-30195 | To Canada |
| F-10 | 2 | 41-30426/-30427 | |

| Designation | Amount | Serial Number(s) | Notes of Interest |
| --- | --- | --- | --- |
| F-10 | 1 | 41-30554 | |
| F-10 | 1 | 41-30580 | |
| F-10 | 2 | 43-3371/-3372 | |
| F-10 | 1 | 43-3416 | |
| F-10 | 1 | 43-3419 | |
| F-10 | 2 | 43-3433/-3434 | |
| F-10 | 4 | 43-3437/-3440 | |
| F-10 | 1 | 43-3444 | |
| F-10 | 1 | 43-3446 | |
| XB-25E | 1 | 42-32281 | Formerly a B-25C-10-NA |
| XB-25F | 1 | | Formerly a B-25C; unknown serial or block numbers |
| B-25G Proto | 1 | 43-32372 | Formerly a B-25C-1-NA |
| B-25G-1-NA | 4 | 42-32384/-32388 | Modified B-25C-15-NA airplanes |
| B-25G-5-NA | 300 | 42-64802/-65101 | |
| B-25G-10-NA | 100 | 42-65102/-65201 | |
| B-25H Proto | 1 | 42-32372 | Formerly a B-25C-10-NA |
| B-25H-1-NA | 300 | 43-4105/-4404 | |
| B-25H-5-NA | 300 | 43-4405/-4704 | One (43-4406) modified to NA-98X airplane |
| B-25H-10-NA | 400 | 43-4705/-5104 | |
| B-25J-1-NC | 235 | 43-3870/-4104 | One (43-4030) modified to RB-25J; used by Gen. Eisenhower and staff officers |
| B-25J-1-NC | 320 | 43-27473/-27792 | |
| B-25J-5-NC | 320 | 43-27793/-28112 | |
| B-25J-10-NC | 110 | 43-28113/-28222 | |
| B-25J-10-NC | 300 | 43-35946/-36245 | |
| B-25J-15-NC | 455 | 44-28711/-29110 | One (44-28945) modified to RB-25J; used by Gen. Arnold and staff officers; Arnold's second RB-25 |
| B-25J-20-NC | 800 | 44-29111/-29910 | |
| B-25J-25-NC | 1,000 | 44-29911/-30910 | One (44-30047) modified to RB-25J; used by NAA personnel; NAA's second RB-25 |
| B-25J-30-NC | 600 | 44-30911/-31510 | One (44-30975) modified to Executive Transport; formerly a PBJ-1J (BuNo 35848) |
| B-25J-30-NC | 190 | 44-86692/-86891 | |
| B-25J-35-NC | 6 | 44-86892/-86897 | |
| B-25J-35-NC | 18 | 45-8801/-8818 | |
| B-25J-35-NC | 4 | 45-8820/-8823 | |
| B-25J-35-NC | 4 | 45-8825/-8828 | |
| B-25J-35-NC | 1 | 45-8832 | |

The following seventy-two B-25J type airplanes were not complete and accepted contractually, according to NAA's Airframe Contract Record, Contracts and Proposals, Report "O," as of 27 July 1956. They were in flyable condition, however, and were included as part of the postwar aircraft termination inventory.

| Designation | Amount | Serial Number(s) |
| --- | --- | --- |
| B-25J-35-NC | 1 | 45-8819 |
| B-25J-35-NC | 1 | 45-8824 |
| B-25J-35-NC | 3 | 45-8829/-8831 |
| B-25J-35-NC | 67 | 45-8833/-8899 |
| Total | 9,889 | |

# *Appendix B*

# PBJ Acquisition Summary

| Designation | USN Bureau Numbers | USAF Serial Numbers | |
|---|---|---|---|
| PBJ-1 (B-25B) | Unknown BuNos, amount, and SerNos | | |
| PBJ-1C (B-25C) | 34998 to 35002 | (5) | 42-64502/-64506 |
| | 35003 to 35022 | (20) | 42-64602/-64621 |
| | 35023 to 35047 | (25) | 42-64708/-64732 |
| PBJ-1D (B-25D) | 35048 to 35072 | (25) | 41-30730/-30754 |
| | 35073 to 35096 | (24) | 42-87157/-87180 |
| | 35098 to 35122 | (25) | 42-87181/-87205 |
| | 35123 to 35147 | (25) | 43-3320/-3344 |
| | 35148 to 35183 | (35) | 43-3570/-3605 |
| | 35184 | (1) | 43-3651 |
| | 35185 | (1) | 43-3655 |
| | 35186 to 35193 | (8) | 43-3771/-3778 |
| | 35196 to 35202 | (7) | 43-3837/-3843 |
| PBJ-1G (B-25G) | 35097 | (1) | 42-65031 |
| PBJ-1H (B-25H) | 35250 to 35251 | (2) | 43-4659/-4660 |
| | 35252 | (1) | 43-4667 |
| | 35253 | (1) | 43-4669 |
| | 35254 to 35256 | (3) | 43-4671/-4673 |
| | 35257 | (1) | 43-4676 |
| | 35258 | (1) | 43-4710 |
| | 35259 | (1) | 43-4656 |
| | 35260 | (1) | 43-4670 |
| | 35261 | (1) | 43-4675 |
| | 35262 to 35279 | (18) | 43-4685/-4702 |
| | 35280 | (1) | 43-4471 |
| | 35281 | (1) | 43-4482 |
| | 35282 | (1) | 43-4492 |
| | 35283 to 35285 | (3) | 43-4542/-4544 |
| | 35286 to 35288 | (3) | 43-4591/-4593 |
| | 35289 to 35291 | (3) | 43-4682/-4684 |
| | 35292 | (1) | 43-4655 |
| | 35293 | (1) | 43-4658 |
| | 35294 to 35296 | (3) | 43-4664/-4666 |
| | 35297 | (1) | 43-4709 |
| | 88872 | (1) | 43-4530 |
| | 88873 | (1) | 43-4638 |
| | 88874 | (1) | 43-4645 |
| | 88875 | (1) | 43-4661 |
| | 88876 | (1) | 43-4703 |
| | 88877 | (1) | 43-4704 |

| Designation | USN Bureau Numbers | USAF Serial Numbers | |
|---|---|---|---|
| | 88878 to 89050 | (172) | 43-4711/-4883 |
| | 89051 | (1) | 43-4705 |
| | 89052 to 89071 | (19) | 43-5028/-5047 |
| PBJ-1J (B-25J) | 35194 to 35195 | (2) | 43-3985/-3986 |
| | 35203 to 35207 | (5) | 43-27511/-27515 |
| | 35208 to 35214 | (7) | 43-27681/-27687 |
| | 35215 to 35221 | (7) | 43-27904/-27910 |
| | 35222 to 35228 | (7) | 43-28174/-28180 |
| | 35229 to 35238 | (10) | 44-28792/-28801 |
| | 35239 to 35248 | (10) | 44-29064/-29073 |
| | 35249 | (1) | 44-29276 |
| | 35798 to 35820 | (22) | 44-30509/-30531 |
| | 35821 to 35824 | (4) | 44-30353/-30356 |
| | 35825 to 35829 | (5) | 44-30693/-30697 |
| | 35830 to 35837 | (8) | 44-30703/-30710 |
| | 35838 to 35840 | (3) | 44-30716/-30718 |
| | 35841 to 35844 | (4) | 44-30961/-30964 |
| | 35845 to 35848 | (4) | 44-30972/-30975 |
| | 35849 to 35860 | (12) | 44-30980/-30991 |
| | 35861 to 35876 | (16) | 44-31089/-31104 |
| | 35877 to 35879 | (3) | 44-30849/-30851 |
| | 35880 | (1) | 44-30856 |
| | 35881 to 35900 | (10) | 44-31277/-31296 |
| | 35901 to 35920 | (20) | 44-31444/-31463 |
| | 38980 to 38988 | (9) | 44-29277/-29285 |
| | 38989 to 38998 | (10) | 44-29290/-29299 |
| | 38999 to 39012 | (14) | 44-29604/-29617 |
| | 64943 to 64948 | (6) | 44-29618/-29623 |
| | 64949 to 64955 | (7) | 44-29788/-29794 |
| | 64956 to 64962 | (7) | 44-29801/-29807 |
| | 64963 to 64968 | (6) | 44-29814/-29819 |
| | 64969 to 64972 | (4) | 44-29510/-29513 |
| | 64973 to 64987 | (15) | 44-29870/-29884 |
| | 64988 to 64992 | (5) | 44-29897/-29901 |
| Known total | | 682 | |

Type totals: PBJ-1 (unknown); PBJ-1C, 60; PBJ-1D, 151; PBJ-1G, 1; PBJ-1H, 236; and PBJ-1J, 244.

*Author's notes:* 1) The USMC via the USN might have received as many as twenty-four PBJ-1 (B-25B) aircraft (unknown USN Bureau Numbers, USAF Serial Numbers). If this is the correct amount (there is no documentation to this), then procurement of all PBJ-type aircraft would total 706; and 2) The compilation of PBJ-1C through PBJ-1J USN Bureau Numbers and USAF Serial Numbers was provided by Mr. Norman L. Avery in a letter to the author.

*Appendix C*

# B-25 Model Number, Designation, Block Number, and Production Facility

| Model Number | Designation, Block Number, and Production Facility | |
|---|---|---|
| NA-62 | B-25-NA | (NA denotes Inglewood, CA) |
| NA-62A | B-25A-NA | |
| NA-62B | B-25B-NA | |
| NA-82 | B-25C-NA | |
| NA-82 | B-25C-1-NA | |
| NA-90 | B-25C-5-NA | |
| NA-94 | B-25C-10-NA | |
| NA-93 | B-25C-15-NA | |
| NA-96 | B-25C-20-NA | |
| NA-96 | B-25C-25-NA | |
| NA-87 | B-25D-NC | (NC denotes Kansas City, KS) |
| NA-87 | B-25D-1-NC | |
| NA-87 | B-25C-5-NC | |
| NA-87 | B-25D-10-NC | |
| NA-87 | B-25D-15-NC | |
| NA-100 | B-25D-20-NC | |
| NA-100 | B-25D-25-NC | |
| NA-100 | B-25D-30-NC | |
| NA-100 | B-25D-35-NC | |
| NA-94 | XB-25E-NA | |
| NA-94 | XB-25F-NA | |
| NA-94 | B-25G-NA Prototype | |
| NA-95 | B-25G-1-NA | |
| NA-96 | B-25G-5-NA | |
| NA-96 | B-25G-10-NA | |
| NA-94 | B-25H-NA Prototype | |
| NA-98 | B-25H-1-NA | |
| NA-98 | B-25H-5-NA | |
| NA-98X | B-25H-5-NA | (Prototype for R-2800 Double Wasp engines with other modifications) |
| NA-98 | B-25H-10-NA | |
| NA-108 | B-25J-1-NC | |
| NA-108 | B-25J-5-NC | |
| NA-108 | B-25J-10-NC | |
| NA-108 | B-25J-15-NC | |
| NA-108 | B-25J-20-NC | |
| NA-108 | B-25J-25-NC | |
| NA-108 | B-25J-30-NC | |
| NA-108 | B-25J-35-NC | |

# Allied Forces Users—World War II and Foreign Users—Postwar

| User (World War II) | User (Postwar) |
| --- | --- |
| Australia | Argentina |
| Brazil | Bolivia |
| Canada | Chile |
| China | Columbia |
| Great Britain | Cuba |
| The Netherlands | Dominican Republic |
| Russia | Mexico |
| | Peru |
| | Uruguay |
| | Venezuela |

# *Appendix E*

# **Other B-25 Derivatives**

| Designation | Notes of Interest |
|---|---|
| AT-24C | Advanced Trainer; survivors were redesignated TB-25C on 11 June 1948; TB meaning Training Bomber |
| AT-24A | Survivors were redesignated TB-25D on 11 June 1948 |
| AT-24B | Survivors were redesignated TB-25G on 11 June 1948 |
| AT-24D | Survivors were redesignated TB-25J on 11 June 1948 |
| F-10 | Reconnaissance/Photographic; survivors were redesignated RB-25 on 11 June 1948; RB meaning Reconnaissance Bomber |
| CB-25J | Cargo Bomber version of the first of three RB-25J; later redesignated VB-25J (see below); C meaning Cargo/Passenger Transport |
| JB-25J | J meaning Special Test |
| JTB-25J | Special Test/Training version of J model |
| JTB-25N | Special Test/Training version of TB-25N (see below) |
| RB-25 | Surviving F-10 aircraft were redesignated RB-25 on 11 June 1948 |
| TB-25C | Formerly AT-24C (see above) |
| TB-25D | Formerly AT-24A (see above) |
| TB-25G | Formerly AT-24B (see above) |
| TB-25J | Formerly AT-24D (see above) |
| TB-25K | Trainer for Hughes E-1 Radar/Fire Control System |
| TB-25L | Multiengine pilot training/transition aircraft |
| TB-25M | Trainer for Hughes E-5 Radar/Fire Control System |
| TB-25N | Multiengine pilot training/transition aircraft |
| VB-25J | VIP transport version of J model |
| VB-25N | VIEP transport version of N model |
| Mitchell I | British B-25Bs |
| Mitchell II | British B-25Cs and B-25Ds |
| Mitchell III | British B-25Js |

*Authors note:* Hayes Aircraft Company, Birmingham, Alabama, records show that it modified a large number of B-25Js for postwar purposes and, after modification, created the following: six JB-25Js, five JTB-25Js, three JTB-25Ns, ninety-eight TB-25Js, ninety TB-25Ks, seventy-nine TB-25Ls, thirty-five TB-25Ns, six VB-25Js, and twenty-seven VB-25Ns.

# Bibliography

## Periodical Articles

Avery, Norman L. "North American's B-25 Transports." *Journal American Aviation Historical Society*, Summer 1977.

Bernstein, Marc D. "Naval Aviation in WW II: The Early Carrier Raids." *Naval Aviation News*, March-April 1992.

Dean, Jack. "Gun Ship." *Air Classics*, Jul, 1967.

———— "The Flying Gun." *Wings*, August 1993.

Gault, Owen. "Anatomy of a Killer: The Mitchell." *Air Classics*, December 1972.

Lawless, Barbara J. "Raider Reflections." *All Hands*, July 1992.

Mizrahi, Joseph V. "The Prince of Smooth Air." *Airpower*, March 1992.

Reed, Boardman C. "North American Aviation Bombers I Have Known and Flown." *Journal American Aviation Historical Society*, Winter, 1992.

## Books

Avery, Norman L. *B-25 Mitchell: The Magnificent Medium*. St. Paul, MN: Phalanx Publishing, 1992.

Fahey, James C. *US Army Aircraft 1908-1946*. New York: Ships and Aircraft, 1946.
————. *USAF Aircraft 1947-1956*. Dayton, OH: Air Force Museum Foundation, 1978.

Goldberg, Alfred. *A History of the United States Air Force 1907-1957*. Princeton, NJ: D. Van Nostrand Company, The Air Force Association, 1957.

Hickey, Lawrence J. *Warpath Across the Pacific*. Boulder, CO: International Research and Publishing Corporation, October,1989.

Kohn, Leo J. *Pilot's Manual for B-25 Mitchell*. Appleton, WI: Aviation Publications, 1978.

Maurer, Maurer. *World War II Combat Squadrons of the United States Air Force*. Woodbury, NY: Platinum Press, 1992.

McDowell, Ernest R. *B-25 Mitchell in Action*. Carrollton, TX: Squadron/Signal Publications, 1978.

Wagner, Ray. *American Combat Planes*. Garden City, NY: Doubleday, 1982.

## Military/Manufacturer Histories

North American Aviation, Inc., NA-48-971; A Brief History of the B-25 Mitchell Bomber, 1948.

57th Bomb Wing Association, The B-25 over the Mediterranean, 50th Anniversary, 1992.

# Index